THE BIOGRAPHY OF
A CHURCH

ETCHING BY SAMUEL CHAMBERLAIN

THE BIOGRAPHY OF A CHURCH

*A Brief History of Christ Church
Cambridge, Massachusetts*

by

GARDINER M. DAY

Privately Printed at
The Riverside Press
CAMBRIDGE, MASS.
1951

PRINTED IN THE U.S.A.

Dedicated in gratitude

to the memory

of

Mary Deane Dexter

1870–1950

Devoted Member and Historiographer

of the Parish

RECTORS OF CHRIST CHURCH

Missionary and Rector

1. EAST APTHORP 1759–1764
2. THE REV. MR. SAMUEL GRIFFITH   –1765
3. WINWOOD SERJEANT 1767–1774

From the summer of 1774 until the fall of 1790, the Church was closed.

From 1790 until 1829 services were conducted by temporary clergymen and lay-readers.[1]

4. THOMAS W. COIT   April 1829–March 1834
5. MARK ANTONY DeWOLFE HOWE   September 1835–July 1836
6. THOMAS H. VAIL   March 1837–February 1839
7. NICHOLAS HOPPIN   December 1839–June 1874 [2]
8. WILLIAM CHAUNCEY LANGDON   January 1876–November 1878
9. JAMES FIELD SPALDING   December 1879–December 1891
10. WILLIAM BENJAMIN BASIL KING   September 1892–October 1900
11. PRESCOTT EVARTS   December 1900–May 1929
12. CHARLES LESLIE GLENN   March 1930–September 1940
13. GARDINER MUMFORD DAY   June 1941–

[1] The list of temporary ministers and lay readers will be found at the end of Chapter V.

[2] He served as minister in charge from December 1839 until he accepted his election as Rector in June 1843.

CONTENTS

PREFACE

THE LIFE of a human being when viewed from the perspective of time commonly divides itself into such phases as the youthful and the more mature years, the unmarried and the married periods, the military and the civilian years or the times of failure and the times of success. Similarly, the life story of a parish is marked by distinct periods differing one from the other quite as strikingly as do the phases of an individual's life. This book is the biography of a church, and from it emerges the clear personality of Christ Church parish.

As the morale of a ship's crew depends in a large measure upon the personality and competence of the captain, so the esprit de corps of a parish is determined primarily by the character and ability of its rector. The parish chooses its rector. As the years pass, it may be happy in its choice and, giving him loyal support, become a spiritual Gibraltar, or it may regret its choice and falling into a slough of acrimonious division stand still or even be thrown into retreat. Who can tell what diverse experiences may befall it?

I became interested in the history of Christ Church parish not simply because I am its thirteenth rector, nor simply because it is an old historic parish of which it could be said "George Washington slept here," but because I became intrigued by the amazingly different types of men who were its rectors and the resulting extraordinary changes of fortune it experienced.

The first rector, finding controversy with the Puritans uncomfortably hot, chose a quieter ministry in rural England. A Tory rector fled in the face of Yankee rebels. One of the early rectors had forged ordination certificates and ended in jail! The congregation forced two other rectors to resign, one after thirty-five years of service! One rector became a convert to Rome, while blindness compelled another to resign and become a novelist. Only one rector, Dr. Prescott Evarts, enjoyed a long and happy ministry and died peacefully in retirement. The twelfth and thirteenth rectors are still living. In addition, for more than half a century the church had no rector. Used for a time as an army barracks, for sixteen years it stood abandoned, and for more than thirty years it was dependent upon lay readers for its services.

The more one reads of its extraordinary history, the more one is amazed not only that the beautiful colonial church building has survived and is now the oldest church building in Cambridge, but that the spirit of the parish survived and that it has become one of the strongest in the Diocese of Massachusetts.

I have tried to narrate the history as a story and at the same time record facts about the past which presumably would be of interest to members and friends of the parish today and in the years ahead. I hope that those who read this volume may enjoy a measure of the fascination that I enjoyed in piecing the story together from the parish records.

I wish to indicate my very great indebtedness to two volumes on the history of Christ Church. The first is a book published in 1858 containing "An Historical Notice of Christ Church" and four historical sermons by the seventh rector, the Rev. Nicholas Hoppin. The other is a small historical sketch of the parish written by Samuel F. Batchelder, privately printed in a limited edition in 1893, in which the author devotes sixty pages to the history of the parish from its founding to the year 1840, the remaining five pages covering the fifty-three year period to 1893. I have leaned heavily, as my footnotes indicate, on these two accounts of the first seventy years of the church's history, although at a number of points I have added new material. Lacking the advantage afforded by these two earlier histories, I should almost certainly never have attempted to write this volume.

Anyone interested in the history of the parish will find himself particularly indebted to Mr. Batchelder who, during his twenty-seven years as clerk of the vestry, carefully organized the early records and put them in scrap books for their better preservation.

The information in this history, the source of which is not indicated in the notes, comes from the minutes of parish and vestry meetings and from other documents preserved in the parish archives.

No one could be more aware than I am of the utter impossibility of giving individual mention to the large number of devoted members of the parish who have made vital contributions to its life. Nor will anyone be more surprised than I if some errors are not found in this volume. Any corrections or any significant new information about events or people will be appreciated, and they also will be preserved against that future day when there will be a need for this "Biography of a Church" to be brought up to date.

I am indebted to several members of the parish for reading all or part of the manuscript, but particularly to my wife for her careful proofreading at successive stages in the composition of the book.

G.M.D.

April 5, 1951
Christ Church Rectory
Cambridge, Massachusetts.

THE BIOGRAPHY OF
A CHURCH

CHAPTER I

EAST APTHORP BUILDS THE CHURCH
1759–1764

THE AMERICAN COLONIES, and the New England Colonies
in particular, were not happy hunting grounds for the
missionaries of the Church of England since the colonists
were for the most part dissenters driven by a determination to get away from the Established Church. Nevertheless, as the result of persistent effort King's Chapel, Christ
Church, and Trinity had been established in Boston by
1759, and the following churches in other Massachusetts
communities: Christ Church, Braintree (now Quincy); St.
Paul's, Newburyport; St. Michael's, Marblehead; St.
Thomas', Taunton; St. Andrew's, Scituate (now Han-
over); St. Peter's, Salem; St. Paul's, Hopkinton; Trinity, Bridgewater; and St. Paul's, Dedham, the foundation
of which was laid in 1758.

The beautiful village of Cambridge, well on the way to
becoming the fountainhead of Puritan thought by virtue
of the college recently founded by John Harvard, lay
about five miles from King's Chapel and was reached only
by ferry across the river. In this village there was a small
group of inhabitants who found the long trip every Sunday to Boston increasingly arduous. The members of the
Church of England in Cambridge felt the community
deserved a church and missionary of its own, and so, on
the fifth of April, 1759, they sent the following letter to

East Apthorp.

the Rev. Dr. Bearcroft, Secretary of the Society for the
Propagation of the Gospel in Foreign Parts, which was
the leading missionary organization in the Church of
England:

Reverend Sir:

We the subscribers, for ourselves, and in the name and
at the desire of a considerable number of families professing
the Church of England at Cambridge, Watertown, and
places adjacent, humbly beg leave to represent to the Society the difficulties we labor under in regard to the means of
public worship, and to entreat their charitable assistance.
There is no Church nearer to us than Boston, which is from
some of us eight, from others ten and twelve miles distant;
unless, for shortening the way we submit to the inconven-

ience of crossing a large ferry, which in stormy weather, and in the winter season especially, is very troublesome and sometimes impracticable. The Society will easily conceive the difficulty of conveying whole families to a place of public worship at such a distance, and attended by such obstructions. To remedy which, we have agreed to build a Church at Cambridge, which, as it is in the center, may indifferently serve the neighboring places, of Charlestown, Watertown, and Newtowne; besides providing for the young Gentlemen who are students at the College here, many of whom, as they have been brought up in the Church of England, are desirous of attending the worship of it. We have also made application to Mr. Apthorp, for whom we have a great esteem, and who is willing to undertake the care of such a church, on supposition we can procure him an honourable support. It is for this purpose, we have presumed to apply to the Society, being sensible that without this kind assistance our attempt would be frustrate. For our parts, we purpose and promise, for ourselves and in behalf of those we represent, to provide a Parsonage house and a Glebe, and to pay annually to Mr. Apthorp twenty pounds sterling, if the Society shall think proper to countenance our design, and assist us with such farther provision as may enable him to settle among us. We shall indeed be ready to comply with any farther instructions the Society shall please to communicate within the compass of our ability; and shall make such authentic instruments for accomplishing what we propose, as the Society shall intimate to be proper.

Humbly begging a favourable answer to our request, we take leave to profess that we are, Rev. Sir, the Societies' and your most humble servants.

Henry Vassall	Joseph Lee
John Vassall	Ralph Inman
Thomas Oliver	David Phips
Robert Temple	James Apthorp

This letter was also accompanied by a letter from the rector of King's Chapel in Boston, Dr. Caner, addressed to the Archbishop of Canterbury,[1] not only stating the need but also suggesting to his Grace the name of East Apthorp who had volunteered to go as a missionary to Cambridge.

Mr. Apthorp, the fourth son of Charles Apthorp, Esquire, a prosperous Boston merchant, was born in Boston in 1733. After attending the Boston Latin School, East Apthorp completed his education at Jesus College, Cambridge, England, graduating cum laude, and was chosen a Fellow of his college. He married Elizabeth Hutchinson, sister of the governor of the Colony, in 1759 and that same year, at the age of twenty-six, became the first rector of Christ Church. He was evidently a man who combined learning and piety with a winsome and attractive personality. The Venerable Andrew Burnaby, Archdeacon of Leicester, England, who traveled in the Colonies in 1760, wrote: "The Rev. Mr. Apthorp is a very amiable young man of shining parts, great learning, and pure and engaging manners."[2] Dr. Prescott Evarts described him as "an aristocrat, a scholar, and a gentleman."[3]

Simultaneously, with the sending of the petition to the Society for the Propagation of the Gospel, the committee set out to secure a site, to have plans drawn for a church building, and to raise the necessary funds. The present site was chosen, half of it being purchased from one James Reid, and the other half from "the Proprietors of the Common and Undivided Lands of the Town of Cambridge." Mr. Peter Harrison, who had designed King's Chapel,[4] was a natural choice as the architect. On Sep-

[1] For Dr. Caner's letter, see Appendix A.

[2] Hoppin, Nicholas, *Historical Notice of Christ Church, 1858*, p. 29.

[3] Evarts, P., *A Brief Address on the History of Christ Church*, p. 16.

[4] For further information, see *Peter Harrison, First American Architect* by Carl Bridenbaugh, University of North Carolina Press, 1949.

tember 28, 1759, the building committee voted "that a letter be written to Mr. Harrison of Newport requesting a Plan and Elevation of the Outside and Inside and of the Pulpit and Vestry of the Church; and that, if Mr. Harrison approves of it, there be no steeple, only a Tower with a Belfry, and that he be informed of the dimensions of a picture designed for the Chancel." The further requirements were "that the extreme dimensions of the Church, including the thickness of the Walls, but exclusive of the Chancel and Tower, be Sixty Feet in Length and Forty-five Feet in Breadth, and further that the Architect be at liberty to make any alterations in the above named dimensions of Sixty Feet by Forty-five Feet provided he does not enlarge the Area of the Church and that the Expense of erecting the whole building is not to exceed Five hundred pounds sterling; that the building be of wood, and covered on the outside with Rough-cast; that there be only one tier of windows, and no Galleries, except an organ loft."

Cambridge in 1759

Before continuing our story, let us try to picture Cambridge as it was in 1759. It was a town of about fifteen hundred inhabitants. The following brief description of its appearance is taken from an address delivered at the 150th anniversary celebration in 1911 by Richard H. Dana, president of the Cambridge Historical Society, and a devoted member of the parish:

Cambridge was "a compact, neat, and pretty village. At this time it had just begun to spread in various directions. In the middle of the village, in what we call Harvard Square, stood fine elm trees shading the town pump and watering trough. On the west side of the square stood the court house . . . A little way south, on Boylston Street, was the Blue Anchor Tavern, that played so important a role in the lives of our great grandfathers. . . . This street led to the great or Boylston Street bridge, the only bridge leading to Boston. Professor Wigglesworth lived in the college yard east of the president's house, and beyond that, toward Boston, stood the parsonage, where Dr. Appleton lived. Still further to the east, north of what is now called Massachusetts Avenue, was the large three-story house of Ralph Inman, the only house between the college yard and Boston. . . .

"The Foxcroft house, to the northeast of the square, was a conspicuous mansion. The Apthorp house, popularly called the Bishop's Palace, though no bishop ever lived there, had just been completed on the south side of Massachusetts Avenue between Plympton and Linden Streets. To the west were six large mansions on what was called Tory Row, Church Row, or the King's Highway, now a part of Brattle Street. The John Vassall, Jr., house, now known as the Longfellow house, had just been built two years before. Elmwood was added to the Row a year or two afterward, making the seventh. . . .

"On the site of Christ Church was formerly the village pound. The common, which was opposite the Church, by this time cut down to its present size, was owned by common proprietors who pastured their cows on allotted portions. It was only later that it was transferred to the Town of Cambridge as a training ground. . . .

"The roads were execrable. The dust or mud was worse than in New England generally on account of the nature of the soil and the lack of good binding gravel. It must have taken a good hour and a half to drive the eight miles from Harvard Square by way of the great bridge, Roxbury and the Neck to Boston." [5]

Cambridge's special distinction lay in the fact that Harvard College had been established there in 1636. The college comprised five buildings, Harvard, Stoughton,

[5] Dana, Richard H., *Address at 150th Anniversary*, The Cambridge Tribune, October 21, 1911.

and Massachusetts Halls, Holden Chapel, and the President's House, now known as Wadsworth House. In addition to Edward Holyoke, the President, the college consisted of two professors, four tutors, and a librarian, and about one hundred and eighty students. The undemocratic climate typical of Massachusetts in those days is evidenced by the fact that the names of the students of the college were not printed in the official catalogue in alphabetical order but in accordance with their social rank. Also at this time slavery existed in Massachusetts and the records show that there were slaves in Cambridge.

The life of the community centered in the Meeting House, of which the minister, Dr. Nathaniel Appleton, was in the forty-fourth year of a sixty-year pastorate. The standard of morals, mores, and manners of the community were set by the governing committee of the Meeting House, and so far as possible conformity was made compulsory. For example, in the Meeting House records on May 8, 1761, we read: "By handy vote the same Committee was chosen as was last year to inspect the manner of professing Christians, etc."

The Meeting House naturally dominated the religious life and thought of the community; almost everyone at least nominally belonged to it except some forty people who were members or friends of the Church of England. Fortunately the extreme Calvinism that characterized New England Puritanism at this time had been modified in Cambridge through the liberalizing influences of the college. Nevertheless, as we shall see, the Church of England was feared and disliked as a symbol of the growing tyranny of an increasingly disliked English government and of the "tyranny of the bishops" which had caused the Puritans to flee England for the Colonies. No doubt the fear of the Church of England had been greatly

increased by the conversion of seven Congregational clergymen, including the President of Yale, earlier in the century.

Christ Church.—Cambridge.

AN EARLY ENGRAVING

The Building of the Church

Mr. Apthorp came to Cambridge immediately upon
appointment and worked for the next two years with the
building committee in supervising the construction of the
new church.   He without doubt made a hit with more
than the building committee when he declined to take his
annual salary of £50 during this period and turned it into
the building fund.   The construction of the building was
evidently begun late in the fall of 1759, as there is a
record of the purchase in November, 1759, of ballast
stones from a vessel from Quebec.   These stones were
used as part of the foundation.   The building accounts

show that most of the materials for the edifice were brought up the Charles river from Boston. It is believed that the main timbers, including the eight pillars, were felled in the upper reaches of the river, for payments are recorded for rafting and boating expenses. The pillars were bored to prevent warping-cracks and shaped by machinery either set up on the Common or at a shop which is known to have been located as late as 1798 at the corner of the present Waterhouse Street and Concord Avenue. The pillars were put in place unfinished and the capitals were not carved until 1826.[6] The cornerstone was laid early in 1760. The building was completed and the opening service held in it on Thursday, October 15, 1761, at 11:00 A.M.[7]

Although the building committee had voted that the cost should not be over £500, it actually reached £1300. The very large increase in the estimated cost was probably the reason why the coating of roughcast was never added, the belfry left half completed, and the capitals of the pillars not carved. Many of the furnishings for the new building, such as an organ, for example, were not installed until several years later. Since there was no money to purchase furnishings, it was necessary to wait upon the future generosity of the friends of this newly established church.

It is interesting to note that the cornerstone is not now visible. This has resulted in theories that the stone was stolen by Tories during the Revolution, or that it was removed or destroyed at the time of the enlargement of the church in 1857. However, inasmuch as it was customary in the eighteenth century to place cornerstones

---

[6] *Christ Church, Cambridge. Some account of its present condition* by Samuel F. Batchelder, Clerk of the Vestry, 1900–1927, p. 14. This booklet was privately printed and few copies are known to be in existence at present.

[7] For the beautiful prayer of East Apthorp at the Dedication, slightly revised by Dr. Hoppin in 1861, see Appendix B.

face down in the mortar to preserve the inscription for all time, we may presume that this was done in the case of this cornerstone. Whether it is still there remains to this day an unsolved question.[8]

In 1764, Harvard Hall, which contained the College Library, was completely destroyed by fire. East Apthorp, at the request of the President and Fellows of Harvard College, appealed to the Society for the Propagation of the Gospel for aid in re-establishing the library. In his appeal he notes, "The library and other advantages of the College are distinguishing benefits to this mission, and I am under personal obligations both to the town and the College, for their favors to me." [9] As a result, the Society for the Propagation of the Gospel sent £100 worth of books to the college, and the letter and vote of thanks of the Harvard Corporation stated, "The books you have sent are just such as we wish to have. They were scarce of any of them in the Library before, and will always be an evidence of the learning and judgment of the gentleman who chose them."

The Mayhew Controversy

East Apthorp ministered to the congregation for three years, but they were not happy years because of the considerable opposition to the founding of a mission of the Church of England in Cambridge. The opposition was led by the Rev. Jonathan Mayhew, pastor of the West Church in Boston, who contended that there was no need for Christ Church inasmuch as there were scarcely ten heads of families in Cambridge desirous of attending Christ Church, "five or six of whom are gentlemen of figure, having each, as is supposed, an income large enough

[8] For inscription on the cornerstone, see Appendix C.

[9] Evarts, Prescott, *A Brief History of Christ Church*, Cambridge, p. 16 (Pamphlet now out of print).

to maintain a domestic chaplain." East Apthorp replied (and his reply is substantiated by church records showing the deeds of sales of pews and the treasurer's accounts), "the number of families belonging to the mission was twenty-six with thirty-three communicants, and that the usual attendance in winter was forty to fifty people and in summer seldom fewer than one hundred persons."

The Congregationalists were *the* community in those days. The founding of the mission in Cambridge in the immediate neighborhood of Harvard College and the appointment of so able a man as East Apthorp simply added fuel to the already strong suspicion that the Society for the Propagation of the Gospel was not only dangerous as the advance agency of the Church of England, but was composed of Tories committed to uphold the increasingly hated Crown; and indeed, this suspicion was well founded, for the Society for the Propagation of the Gospel instructed its missionaries to endeavor "with the utmost care and zeal to support their Majesty's government." [10] It was further rumored that East Apthorp had an eye on the episcopate, as it was naturally assumed that eventually bishoprics would be established in the Colonies. This rumor may have arisen because he built for himself a spacious and costly mansion. It still stands between Plympton and Linden Streets and is the residence of the Master of Adams House.[11] Indeed, Dr. Mayhew in one of his pamphlets wrote, "Since the Mission was established in Cambridge, and a very sumptuous dwelling house (for this country) erected there, that town hath been often talked of by the Episcopalians as well as others as the proposed place of residence for a bishop." [12]

[10] Batchelder, S., *ibid.*, p. 27.

[11] The house soon became known as "The Bishop's Palace." It served as General Putnam's headquarters during the battle of Bunker Hill. In 1777 it was the prison house for General Burgoyne and his staff.

[12] Hoppin, *ibid.*, p. 31.

In February, 1763, in the third year of East Apthorp's rectorship, this controversy with Dr. Mayhew broke out afresh. A missionary of the Society for the Propagation of the Gospel who was a rector of a small congregation in

APTHORP HOUSE, NOW THE RESIDENCE OF THE
MASTER OF ADAMS HOUSE

the town of Braintree died. At the time of his death there appeared in public press an article questioning the right and propriety of the Society for the Propagation of the Gospel in England subsidizing a clergyman to hold services in communities such as Braintree which were well provided with Congregational clergy and churches.

East Apthorp wrote a reply to this criticism of his friend and of the Society for the Propagation of the Gospel in the form of a pamphlet entitled *Considerations on the Institution and Conduct of the Society for the Propagation of the Gospel in Foreign Parts.* This was the spark that led to a pamphlet war between East Apthorp and other clergy of the Church of England including the Archbishop of Canterbury on one side, and a number of distinguished Congregationalists on the other. East Apthorp, no doubt to his surprise, to use his own words, "though actuated by the best of motives and a desire to do such service as he could for the Church of England and his country, sustained as rude a storm as perhaps ever beat upon a person of his station." [13] Whether it was that he did not like a fight or felt he was too greatly outnumbered, in any case, when the opportunity of becoming vicar of Croydon, England, was offered to him, East Apthorp left, never to return to the Colonies. "I have heard," says Dr. Burnaby, "that this gentleman met with so much opposition and persecution from the Congregationalists, that he was obliged to resign his Cure, to quit the Colony, and has since lived in England." [14]

It is interesting that some thirty years later when the church was struggling for survival a lay reader who helped to keep its doors open was a grandson of Jonathan Mayhew named Jonathan Mayhew Wainwright, who later became Bishop of New York.

East Apthorp's Later Years

Mr. Apthorp served as vicar of Croyden for twenty-eight years. During this period he devoted himself largely to classical and historical studies. In 1778 he published a volume replying to the attack on Christianity contained in Gibbons' *History of the Decline and Fall of the Roman Empire.* Soon after the appearance of this work Arch-

---

[13] Hoppin, Nicholas, *A Commemorative Sermon*, 1861, p. 24.
[14] Hoppin, Nicholas, *A Historical Notice of Christ Church*, 1858, p. 31.

bishop Cornwallis conferred on him the degree of Doctor of Divinity and appointed him to the rectorship of St. Mary-le-Bow, London. In 1790 he was made a prebendary of St. Paul's Cathedral and about the same time declined an appointment to the bishopric of Kildare because of his failing eyesight. He died in 1817 at the age of 84 and had the honor of being buried in the Chapel of Jesus College, Cambridge.

While the chief credit for the beauty of the church building must go to the architect, Mr. Harrison, nevertheless, the main contribution of East Apthorp to the parish was his planning and supervision of its construction. That he was possessed of artistic appreciation and discriminating taste is witnessed by the fact that he was among the first to recognize the building as an architectural masterpiece and in his sermon at the opening service said:

> "You see a noble undertaking in a great measure performed. . . . This temple hath arisen to the glory of God, and the promoting of Christianity, with a beauty and elegance not unbecoming the majesty of religion. Much has been done already by your munificence toward completing a structure, the least merit of which is the honor it does to our country by adding to the few specimens we have of excellence in the fine arts which, under the conduct of a good imagination, have so much influence in polishing and humanizing the mind, and when employed in the service of religion are so expressive of reverence to the Deity. . . ."

A description of the original church building together with an account of some of the more significant additions and alterations which have been made to it will be found in a supplementary chapter at the close of this "Biography of a Church."

THE TOWER ON A WINTER NIGHT

CHAPTER II

AN IMPOSTOR AND A TORY

1764–1774

THE STORY OF THE SECOND AND THIRD MISSIONARIES

ANYONE WHO desires to volunteer for missionary work in the Church today is not accepted until the proper authorities have satisfied themselves as to his qualifications of character, education, and ability. Until recent times, however, anyone who volunteered for the mission field was automatically accepted on the belief that he had received a call from God, the validity of which it was irreverent to question. Many a clergyman unable to maintain the respect of a congregation at home went to the mission field; and, as in other fields, the Colonies received their share of undesirable ministers. Such a volunteer was the choice of the Society for the Propagation of the Gospel as the second missionary for Christ Church in the person of one Samuel Griffith. He was with the parish for only six months and the records of the parish omit any mention of him except his name.

We are indebted to Dr. Prescott Evarts' research into the history of the parish for our knowledge of what an exciting and intriguing time the parishioners must have had during the winter of 1764–1765, when Mr. Griffith was in charge. The knowledge we have of Mr. Griffith is found in a letter written by Dr. Caner, the rector of King's

Chapel, to the Society for the Propagation of the Gospel explaining why Mr. Griffith had to be dismissed:

"I am sorry to acquaint you that Mr. Griffith (as he called himself) has turned out the most impudent impostor that I have ever known. His name, he now says and possibly with truth, is Mieux, son of Richard Mieux a clergyman now deceased. He is not in orders, but being possessed of Richard Mieux' letters of Orders, had erased the name and altered the date, putting Samuel Griffith, 1762. . . . This very bad man had with him a large number of manuscript sermons. . . . He is but twenty-seven years of age, and sometimes affirms to have been educated at Oxford, and sometimes at Cambridge. . . .

"What occasioned his destruction was his lying and stealing, for both of which he is infamous to a proverb. He has stolen from every house in the Parish where he was intimate, — silver spoons, shirts, a piece of linen, books, rings, a tweezer case of silver, silk, a girdle buckle, umbrellas, napkins, table-cloths, etc. When he found himself discovered, he endeavored to make off, but was taken, and is now in prison, and to have his trial at the sessions in October." [1]

I have no doubt that after this experience both the Society for the Propagation of the Gospel and the congregation became a bit more cautious regarding the securing of a new minister.

Winwood Serjeant

In any case, the church availed itself of the services of a supply minister and a lay reader for a period of two years before it accepted another missionary from the Society for the Propagation of the Gospel. The Rev. William Agar served as a locum tenens from October 1766 until the new missionary, the Rev. Winwood

[1] Evarts, P., *A Brief Address on the History of Christ Church*, p. 19.

Serjeant, arrived as rector in June, 1767. In a letter to the Society for the Propagation of the Gospel, Mr. Agar gives this description of the composition of the congregation: "All the proprietors of the church are men of fortune. Some of the collegians come to church." [2]

Mr. Serjeant, a native of Bristol, England, went as a missionary of the S.P.G. to Charleston, South Carolina in 1756. Finding that the climate did not agree with him, he moved to St. George's parish, Dorchester, where he remained until he came to Christ Church in June, 1767. Concerning Mr. Serjeant, Dr. Nicholas Hoppin writes: "A few of his letters which have been preserved . . . show him to have been of a spritely turn, with a touch of humor and pleasantry, but a man of tender feelings and affectionate disposition." [3] Mr. Samuel Batchelder says "that the eight years of Mr. Serjeant's ministry are among the happiest in the history of the Church." Mr. Serjeant himself wrote to the Society for the Propagation of the Gospel:

> "The Church of Cambridge affords nothing of consequence to communicate, except the happiness of assuring you of its regularity and tranquility. The congregation increases notwithstanding the late loss of two principal families by death and removal. My communicants make a superior figure to most in the country."

Presumably the death referred to is that of Colonel Henry Vassall who died in 1769 and was buried in a tomb which he had prepared beneath the church. [4]

Fortunately for the parish, unlike East Apthorp, Mr. Serjeant was not interested in polemics but rather devoted himself to shepherding his little flock of fifteen or twenty families of whom he wrote: "Six of them possessed of ample fortunes, the rest in very easy circumstances

[2] Hoppin, Nicholas, *A Historical Notice of Christ Church*, p. 39.

[3] Hoppin, Nicholas, *ibid.*, p. 43.

[4] For information concerning the Vassall tomb, see Appendix E.

were retired from business." It was during Mr. Serjeant's rectorship in 1772 that the William and Mary communion service was presented to the church by Governor Hutchinson.[5]

The peace and serenity of Mr. Serjeant's ministry was to be short-lived however, as the autocracy of the King of England, which was to lead to the American Revolution, was becoming continually more severe and unbearable to the people in the Colonies. Mr. Serjeant himself as well as his entire congregation were strong Tories with the exception of two people, John Pigeon and Joseph Lee, who were the only members of the congregation to remain in Cambridge during the Revolution. John Pigeon was a proprietor (vestryman) and the only member of the congregation to espouse the cause of the Colonies, while the Honorable Joseph Lee, Judge of Common Pleas and a member of the Honorable Council, was a neutral in politics who was allowed to remain in the community. The loyalist temper of the congregation was doubly emphasized by the fact that, while the Governor of the Colony attended King's Chapel, the Lieutenant Governor, Thomas Oliver, a Crown appointee, was a prominent member of Christ Church and a Cambridge resident. Mr. Serjeant was bound by his ordination vows to be loyal to the King and the Royal Family and to pray for them at every regular service. Consequently, as the spirit of rebellion waxed more vehement, Mr. Serjeant and his little congregation became in the minds of the native population an increasingly resented symbol of the autocratic power of the English Crown.

In March, 1774, the Rev. Mr. Serjeant wrote:

"The populace are almost daily engaged in riots and tumults. On the 7th inst. they made a second destruction of thirty chests of tea. Political commotions run extremely

[5] For description of the Communion service, see Appendix F.

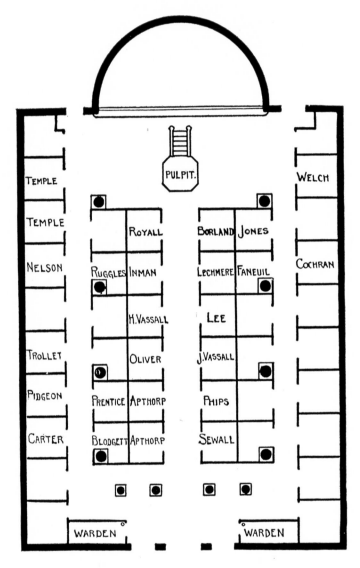

The Tory Proprietors, circa 1770.

high in Boston; if not suppressed soon, the whole province is in danger of being thrown into anarchy and confusion." [6]

In June he writes:

"Boston is in a terrible situation and will be much more so if they do not submit to government before fall; the poor will be most miserably distressed and the town must be absolutely ruined." [7]

During the summer many of the congregation, including Major John Vassall and John Borland, took refuge with the British troops stationed in Boston while Mr. Serjeant and the rest of the congregation fled north, some to Newburyport and others even to Nova Scotia and eventually back to England. Lieutenant Governor Thomas Oliver remained until September, when an armed mob appeared in front of his house and forced him to flee the community.

Dr. Caner of King's Chapel in Boston wrote from Boston to the Society for the Propagation of the Gospel on June 2, 1775:

"Mr. Sergeant of Cambridge has been obliged with his family to fly for the safety of their lives, nor can I learn where he is concealed. His fine church is turned into a barracks by the rebels, and a beautiful organ that was in it broke to pieces." [8]

Mr. Serjeant's experience was typical of that endured by all but two members of the congregation. In August, 1775, Mr. Serjeant wrote:

"Families, however inoffensive, suspected to retain any loyal principles, (were) treated with the utmost insolence and rigor. I was obliged to retreat with my family fifty miles into the country to Kingston, in New Hampshire, where I was in hopes of meeting with a peaceful retirement among rural peasants, but my hopes were soon disappointed.

[6] Batchelder, Samuel, *History of Christ Church*, 1893 (privately printed), p. 36.
[7] *Ibid.*   [8] Hoppin, *ibid.*, p. 42.

The restless spirit of fanaticism renders unintelligent minds more licentious. I found it necessary to remove to Newbury, where I hoped to be protected from the insults of the common people. I have lost not less than £300 in household furniture and books destroyed and pillaged." [9]

Mr. Weeks, a clergyman in Marblehead, wrote in 1778: "Mr. Serjeant's parish at Cambridge is wholly broken up. The elegant houses of those gentlemen who once belonged to it are now occupied by the rebels, and Mr. Inman, a man of fortune and figure, is now obliged to purchase things from his own farm at Cambridge. The rebels have taken from him everything except his wearing apparel, only because he had been one of the King's Council in that province." [9]

From Kingston, Mr. Serjeant went to Newburyport, where he lived until he was stricken with paralysis in 1777. The following year he returned with his family to Bristol, England, where he lingered until a stroke ended his life in 1780.

[9] Hoppin, *ibid.*, p. 43.

Two Views of the Gallery and Southeast Corner
where the Baptistry is now Located

CHAPTER III

THE CHURCH DURING THE REVOLUTION

1775–1790

AFTER THE RECTOR and congregation of Christ Church fled in the summer of 1774, the church saw no regular services for 16 years. Nevertheless, in addition to being used as a barracks for Colonial troops during this period, the most famous single service ever held in the church, the New Year's Eve service in 1775 for General and Mrs. Washington, took place, as well as a funeral service in 1778 that had most disastrous consequences for the church.

John Pigeon, the sole Yankee proprietor, was appointed Commissary General to the Provincial Forces, and he could hardly have had much time to concern himself with the care and protection of the building. Soon after the battles of Lexington and Concord in April, 1775, Colonial soldiers began to arrive in Cambridge. The four buildings of Harvard College were used as barracks but they were not sufficient to quarter all the troops. Therefore, General Artemus Ward, who was in command of the Provincial Forces, had assigned Christ Church as a barracks for a company of volunteers from Wethersfield, Connecticut, under the command of Captain John Chester. Although the metal organ pipes and window-sash weights were removed and made into bullets by the Connecticut Yankees, Samuel Batchelder states: "The greater part of the damage that the Church sustained at this period was not inflicted by Captain Chester's Company." [1] During the Revolution, the church was marred by a number of bullet holes, such as the one now marked by a plaque in the porch of the church. Even Mr. Batchelder admits, however, that the bullet hole on the porch may very likely have been the result of a shot by one of these Yankee soldiers rather than by a British soldier! (Actually, there is no evidence from the records one way or the other, but who would have dared put up a sign saying it had been an American soldier!) It is interesting to note that in the battle of Bunker Hill, Captain Chester was mentioned with special credit. Happily, by early December the Wethersfield Company was able to withdraw from the church to permanent barracks, and the church again stood boarded up and abandoned.

George Washington at Christ Church

General Washington arrived in Cambridge on the afternoon of July 2, 1775, and took up his residence in the Vassall house (now 105 Brattle Street). He naturally worshipped with the rest of the community in the Congregational Meeting House, whose pastor was the Rev. Nathaniel Appleton. General Washington was, however, a baptized member of the Church of England. Mrs. Washington evidently was the more ardent member of the Established Church. She arrived in Cambridge on December 11th, for in the diary of Dorothy Dudley on December 18th, we read, "Mrs. Washington has expressed a wish that Christ Church may be put in readiness for services, and orders have gone forth to that effect." [2] As New Year's Eve fell on Sunday, and inasmuch as there

---

[1] Batchelder, *ibid.*, p. 39.

[2] The Cambridge of 1776 with the Diary of Dorothy Dudley edited for the Ladies Centennial Committee, Cambridge, 1875, p. 49.

was no artificial light in the church, we assume that this service was held at the usual hour of worship Sunday morning, namely, eleven o'clock. The accounts of the service indicate that General and Mrs. Washington occupied Robert Temple's pew, being the third from the front on the left side of the church. Samuel Batchelder suggests that "this pew may have been assigned to them as being the cleanest and least injured of any." [3] General Washington was accompanied by his staff and general officers, along with their wives and families. In the absence of a clergyman, Colonel William Palfrey of General Washington's staff read the service, and thus describes his performance in a letter to his wife:

> "What think you of my turning parson? I, yesterday, at the request of Mrs. Washington, performed divine service at the Church at Cambridge.
> "There was present the General and lady, Mrs. Gates, Mrs. Curtis, and a number of others, and they were pleased to compliment me on my performance. I made a form of prayer, instead of the prayer for the king, which was much approved." [4]

Colonel Palfrey prayed that God might open the eyes of King George III, and enlighten his understanding so that he would learn to pursue the true interests of the people over whom he ruled. He also asked God's blessing on the Continental Congress and, of course, on the Commander-in-Chief of the American Forces. [5]

Dorothy Dudley comments on the service in her diary under the date of January 1, 1776, "General and Mrs. Washington, Mrs. Gates, Mrs. Morgan, Mrs. Mifflin, Mrs. Curtis, and many others, including officers, were present. . . . There was something grand and yet incongruous in the service in this church, which has so lately

---

[3] Batchelder, *ibid.*, p. 42.   [4] *Ibid.*, p. 42.
[5] For the complete prayer, see Appendix G.

sheltered the rollicking soldiers. Doors shattered and windows broken out, organ destroyed, and the elegance and beauty of the building greatly marred. It has been imperfectly repaired at the request of one whom its former aristocratic worshippers hold in supreme contempt as a rebel against his Majesty's most righteous rule." [6] (This rebel was undoubtedly the loyal John Pigeon.)

The Description of an Eyewitness

Inasmuch as this service is of more general interest than any other service held in Christ Church, we quote the following excerpt from a letter written by Lydia Biddle of Philadelphia to Mrs. Sarah Morris Mifflin, also of Philadelphia. Mrs. Mifflin was the wife of Major Mifflin, who was with the Colonial troops in Cambridge. Evidently Lydia Biddle was visiting in Cambridge and, having the opportunity of witnessing this unique service, wrote an account of it to Mrs. Mifflin in order that she might know not only about the service but about the part which her husband played in it. Part of the letter is as follows:

"General Washington now occupies the stately house which Colonel John Vassall built and some of the medical officers that of his uncle, Henry Vassall. Mrs. Morgan (evidently the daughter of old Thomas Sherren, once Sexton and Clerk of Christ Church), and when she is waiting upon me she amuses me with relating the grand doings of this family — their slaves, their chariots of four black horses, their silver plate and stiff brocades, their grand manners to the college and village people, and above and beyond all the English Church where they meet on Sunday and of which her father was one of the officers. She told me last week that Mrs. Washington was to have the Church cleaned, ready for service and that her brother-in-law, Joseph Welch, who was sexton when the Tories left, and

[6] Dudley, *ibid.*, p. 49.

has the linen and prayer books in his possession has orders from the general to direct a squad of soldiers to clean it out. So Phoebe is in high glee that her brother-in-law has got his own again, as it were, and can make the dirty soldiers repair all they have defaced.

"I hear that the only Churchmen of importance left are Mr. Joseph Lee, a sort of neutral in politics, and Mr. John Pigeon who were both Vestrymen at the beginning of the war. The latter is a patriot, but not of the grand old family — rather a newcomer I think. These two gentlemen waited upon Major Mifflin on Saturday to request him to enter the Church — next in order to the Commander-in-Chief, because in 1762, the year after the Church was opened, thy husband gave the sum of thirteen pounds towards the building. Mr. Lee was very gracious and complimentary to the Major and said he had often heard his cousin Vassall speak of the hospitalities he had received in Philadelphia from the Mifflin family and he should be glad now to return them. The major said when he gave the money he never expected to see the Church and it reminded him of the words of Holy Writ — 'Cast thy bread upon the waters and after many days it shall return to thee again'. . .

". . . Sunday dawned bright and cold as New Year's eve should, and dear Mrs. Morgan who is kindness itself, said, as the back of the Church is almost in our front yard, that we might walk over the frozen snow, cross the lawn and enter the Vestry room door, and see the procession come in. The bell rang at an early hour to give notice of the opening. We put on some warm wraps and moccasins over our shoes and sallied forth. The officers had gone up to headquarters to escort General Washington.

"We opened the Vestry room door and entered softly. I was glad to see a brazier of charcoal burning there for my hands were cold from the frosty air. Joseph Welch who was attending to it gave us a pleasant word of welcome. He was in ecstasies of delight that Mrs. Washington had ordered the Church to be opened, and told us that he con-

sidered it a sacred duty to guard its walls in the absence of
the proprietary, and had wept over its desecration by our
Soldiers.

"The Church is small with four rows of square pews in
the body and a row of wall pews on either side. These latter, raised a foot from the floor, were reserved for the officers, the middle aisles for the civilians and ladies, and the
pews entered from the side aisles for the soldiers. There
are no galleries, but a handsome organ loft supported by
pillars. A row of pillars divide the Nave from the aisles
but they are square and uncarved. Welch said that when
the War broke out, money was being raised to have the
wood handsomely carved — the Church will then be vastly
pretty. Now it reminds one of some building in rural England, as it has a good site opposite the common — square,
we should call it. The Sexton took us to Mr. Henry Vassall's pew No. 3 he said, but I could see no number. All
have perhaps been taken off by the soldiers who used the
place as barracks. Soon after, Mrs. Washington, Mrs.
Gates and Mrs. Curtis entered together and were shown to
a seat in front of us, the Royal pew, Welch said. Do you
think the name prophetic? Our Queen looked very well in
peach-colored satin which is worn on all State occasions
and she glanced most kindly upon us, wishing us 'the
compliments of the season' in quite an audible tone.

"Soon we heard the sound of fife and drum and knew
that the commander-in-chief was approaching. The two
Vestrymen or wardens whom I have mentioned before
stood facing the middle door, with wands of office in hand,
crossed, ready to escort General Washington to his place.
As he entered they each made a most stately bow, which
was returned with his usual courtesy. They preceded him
up the east aisle to a pew within two of the Vestry door.
Major Mifflin walked by his side as had been arranged and
took the seat of honor next him; then followed a long row
of officers in their best uniforms, for every one who could be
spared from duty had been requested to be present. The
body-guard of our chief stood around him and threw their

shakos rather irreverently we thought, on the window sills.

"The soldiers, a company of whom were present, grounded their arms and nothing was heard save the shuffling feet of the Negroes in the background, the former slaves of the Tories who had often come here with their masters in days gone by. The clerk brought out the huge prayer books given by the Honorable Thomas Lechmere and found the places, putting in long purple and gold markers, and Mr. Palfrey, the chaplain, read service. He had composed a prayer instead of that in use for the King, and we thought it very good. The townspeople wondered if King George would be prayed for as usual. Unfortunately the organ could not be used. Some of the leaden pipes had been taken out to furnish ammunition for our men at the fight in Charlestown last June, and it was quite out of order, but a bass viola and clarionet played by some musical soldiers led the singing which was very good. The strong voices of the many men who thronged the Church made fine music for my ears, and when part of Psalm CXVIII and a verse from Psalm CXIX was rolled out I saw some tearful eyes. . . .

"The service was long, but it was delightful to me, and as I sat in the square pew with my back to the Chancel I could just peep over the top as I used to do at St. Peter's in your dear town, when I was visiting Uncle Biddle last year. I could not keep from watching General Washington's serious face, and their stiff wardens who ever and anon took up their wands to tap a noisy urchin standing under the organ loft or a colored boy who was unattentive. Mr. Lee looked as if better days were dawning. We stole out as we had come, through the Vestry room, to avoid the crowd and officers."

Lydia Biddle was evidently not a patriot, as she closes the letter with the following sentence:

"You know where my heart is fixed, and yesterday seeing the empty places of his friends, I am half inclined to go

over to the enemy and leave these thirteen Colonies for-
ever. But dear Sallie, you will not blame me or call it trea-
son in your ever faithful friend." [7]

While Dorothy Dudley in her diary does not give an
extensive account of the service, she contrasts the congregation at the service with the congregation she had
known years before the Revolution in such an interesting
manner that her remarks give us a particularly valuable
picture of earlier and happier years.

"How very different was the scene from that in the days
before the war. The General's majestic figure, bent rever-
ently in prayer, as with devout earnestness he entered into
the service; the smallness of the band of worshippers, and
the strangeness of the circumstances and the surroundings.
There was nothing but the contrast to recall the wealth and
fashion which were wont to congregate there. I remember
the families as they used to sit in church. First, in front of
the chancel were the Temples, who every Sabbath drove
from Ten Hills Farm; Mr. Robert Temple and his accomplished wife and lovely daughters. Their estate, which is a
very fine one, is on the supposed site of Governor Win-
throp's house as early as 1631, and where, it is thought, the
little bark, the Blessing of the Bay, the first vessel built in
American waters, was launched for its first voyage across
the ocean. Mr. Temple is a stanch loyalist, and at the beginning of war took passage for England, leaving his family
at the Farm under General Ward's protection. The vessel,
however, was detained, and he obliged to take up his residence in our camp. Behind the Temples sat the Royalls,
relatives of Mrs. Henry Vassall, the Inmans and the Bor-
lands, who owned and occupied the Bishop's Palace, as the
magnificent mansion, built by Rev. Mr. Apthorp, opposite
the president's house, is called. The house is grand in pro-
portions and architecture, and is fitted in every respect to
bear the name which clings to it. It was thought that Mr.

[7] *Boston Daily Advertiser*, Jan. 1st issue, 1876, p. 1.

Apthorp had an eye to the bishopric when he came to take charge of Christ Church, and put up this house of stately elegance. But whatever his wishes may have been, they were not realized, for he abruptly terminated his ministry in Cambridge after a few years. Among his congregation were the Faneuils, the Lechmeres, the Lees, the Olivers, the Ruggleses, the Phipses, and the Vassalls. Many of these families were connected by relationship. Mrs. Lee, Mrs. Lechmere, and Mrs. Vassall the elder, are sisters of Colonel David Phips, and daughters of Lieutenant-Governor Spencer Phips. The "pretty little, dapper man, Colonel Oliver," as Reverend Mr. Serjeant used to call in sport our sometime lieutenant-governor, married a sister of Colonel John Vassall the younger, and Colonel Vassall married his. Mrs. Ruggles and Mrs. Borland are aunts of Colonel Vassall's. These families were on intimate terms with one another, and scarcely a day passed that did not bring them together for social pleasures. Judge Jonathan Sewall, who afterwards occupied Judge Richard Lechmere's house, married a daughter of Mr. Edmund Quincy, an elder sister of Mrs. John Hancock. I well remember the train of carriages that rolled up to the church door, bearing the worshippers to the Sabbath service. The inevitable red cloak of Judge Joseph Lee, his badge of office in the King's service hung in graceful folds around his stately form; the beauty and elegance of the ladies were conspicuous, as silks and brocades rustled at every motion, and India shawls told of wealth and luxury. The ties of blood and friendship were strengthened by those of a common faith, and the treasury of the church was filled by cheerful givers from their abundance. Now everything is changed — all who took such deep interest in the welfare of the church, all the original subscribers for the building are gone, with exception of Judge Joseph Lee, who is unmolested on account of his moderate principles, and Mr. John Pigeon, who is a patriot." [8]

[8] Dudley, *ibid.*, pp. 50–51. (Ten Hills Farm is now part of Somerville.)

A Unique Funeral Service

Following the evacuation of Boston in March, 1776, and the consequential departure of the Continental Army, Cambridge saw no military activity until November, 1777, when the captured Hessian and British troops numbering 4200 were brought to Cambridge to be kept in the old barracks, built for the besiegers of Boston, as prisoners of war.

One of the saddest episodes in the history of Christ Church occurred when Lieutenant Richard Brown, one of the English prisoners, was driving down what was probably Avon Hill and lost control of his horses. The American sentry challenged him to halt. When Lieutenant Brown was unable to do so, the sentry, not realizing what was happening, shot Lieutenant Brown through the head. This regrettable incident naturally aroused the sympathy of the community. By the consent of General Heath, commanding the guard in Cambridge, Christ Church was allowed to be opened for the funeral service for Lieutenant Brown on June 19, 1778. It was attended by many English officers and soldiers as well as by many of the German officers and by some Americans.

The body of Lieutenant Brown was believed to have been interred in the Vassall tomb in the crypt of the church. During the interment the town folk entered the building and virtually wrecked the interior. Samuel Batchelder says that more damage was done to it on this occasion than it had received during the entire war period. The following is the description of the ransacking of the church as quoted by Samuel Batchelder from Ensign Anbury's "Travels":

"I cannot pass over the littleness of mind, and the pitiful resentment of the Americans, in a very trifling circumstance, (for) during the time the service was performing over the body (at the tomb in the cellar?), the Americans seized the opportunity of the Church being open, which had been shut since the commencement of hostilities, to plunder, ransack and deface every thing they could lay their hands on, destroying the pulpit, reading-desk and communion-table, and ascending the organ loft, destroyed the bellows and broke all the pipes of a very handsome instrument." [9]

Parts of the organ were found in various parts of Cambridge for a long time after this desecration.

After this incident the church building again stood abandoned. As we close the story of this period of what Samuel Batchelder calls Christ Church's era of "desecration and neglect," we may well quote his own description:

"The building was little better than a ruin, 'the doors shattered and all the windows broken out, exposed to rain and storms and every sort of depredation, its beauty gone, its sanctuary defiled, the wind howling through its deserted aisles and about its stained and decaying walls; the whole building being a disgrace instead of an ornament to the town.' The congregation was as completely shattered as the church. Of the whole band of worshippers only John Pigeon and Judge Lee remained in Cambridge. . . . [10]

And so the Christ Church building stood all but neglected and all but forgotten until 1790.

[9] *Ibid.*, Batchelder, p. 46 (from Ensign Anbury's *Travels*, Vol. II, p. 234).
[10] *Ibid.*, p. 47.

CHAPTER IV

THE READING PERIOD

1790–1839

BY THE YEAR 1790, no service had been held in Christ Church in twelve years and no regular services for sixteen years. The building stood like a monumental shell in the heart of Cambridge. It had no congregation and no minister. Of the sixty-eight original subscribers to the building and the twenty original purchasers of pews, the only names to appear on the parish records after the Revolution are those of John Pigeon, Esq., and Judge Joseph Lee. As we have seen, the former was a patriot, while the latter, though a loyalist, had been so moderate in his opinions as to remain unmolested. Judge Lee died in 1802 at the age of 93.

Fortunately, some of the Episcopalians living in Boston, cognizant of the value of preserving the church from an architectural as well as from a religious point of view and encouraged by the Rev. Samuel Parker, rector of Trinity Church, Boston, initiated a subscription for the restoration of the church building. The circular appealing for funds indicated that "in the course of the late War the Church had been much damaged, the windows being totally destroyed, the Pews, Altar and Pulpit exceedingly injured, and the Organ wholly torn to pieces." The appeal was successful, the restoration of the church was carried out, and on July 14, 1790, the church was dedicated and set apart "to the solemn and public worship of Almighty God."

Opening and dedicating the church, however, did not produce a congregation, nor did it produce funds for the

FROM THE MASSACHUSETTS MAGAZINE IN 1792

payment of a minister. The popular feeling evidently remained strong against the Church of England and the things it symbolized. The church for the next thirty-nine years, or until the coming of the Rev. Thomas W. Coit, D.D., as rector in 1829, was to be dependent for services upon a few itinerant clergymen and a great many lay readers.

Worthy of mention is the fact that Elbridge Gerry and Jonathan Simpson, Jr., were elected delegates to represent the parish at the first General Convention of the Protestant Episcopal Church in America.

During the seven years following the reopening of the church in 1790, four clergymen and three lay readers conducted the services, but the wardens and vestrymen were not able to persuade any one of the clergymen to throw in his lot permanently with the parish. From Easter 1796 until December 1797 the reader was Mr. Theodore Dehon, who in 1812 became Bishop of South Carolina. For eight years, from 1797 to 1805, Mr. William Jenks, who later became a Congregational minister, served as the reader with a salary of two hundred and forty dollars a year, but even the sale of pews at an auction failed to save the church from increasing debt.

In 1807, for no accountable reason, the parish suddenly blossomed into new life. The records say that all the pews except three or four were rented, and the following year the services of a clergyman, the Rev. Asa Eaton, rector of Christ Church, Boston, who agreed to preach once every two months, were secured. Most amazing of all, one thousand two hundred and fifty dollars was contributed by the church toward the support of the first Bishop of Massachusetts. The prosperity was unfortunately of a most temporary sort, for by 1809 the church again had only a lay reader. During the next fifteen years the flickering spark of spiritual life was kept alive by eight lay readers until a clergyman was at last secured in the person of the Rev. George Otis in 1824. The dire straits into which the parish had fallen and the methods which were used to remedy it are thus described by Samuel Batchelder:

> "The poverty of the parish had now (1823) reached such a point that only two hundred dollars could be raised for the support of public worship and all other expenses, and the wardens were instructed to supply a reader 'as far as it shall be practicable with the means provided.' It was in this darkest hour of the parish's history that the 'Wardens' Fund' was begun, now the most important source of revenue the church possesses. The women of the parish, in the

year 1820, subscribed and collected the sum of four hundred dollars and ninety six cents 'as a fund towards the support of a settled minister.' A society of Harvard students, the Δειπνόφαγοι, or Dinner-eaters, being on the point of dissolution, generously contributed to this fund the contents of their treasury, two hundred and sixty-five dollars. Other subscriptions raised the amount to over eight hundred dollars. The sum total was received by the wardens 'to be put out to interest on good security, until said Society (the Episcopal Church at Cambridge) shall settle a regularly ordained minister. And at all times hereafter when said fund shall be continued as an increasing fund; but whenever said Society shall have such minister settled with them, the one half of the annual income of the whole fund for the time being shall be appropriated towards his support, and the other half shall go to increase the fund." [1]

The plight of the parish was so serious that regular services had to be discontinued in 1822 and 1823. So disgraceful was this for the reputation of the Diocese that in 1824 a committee was appointed by the Diocese of Massachusetts to solicit subscriptions for repairing the building, which during this "reading period" had fallen into a bad state of disrepair. The appeal was for a fund of three thousand dollars, which was raised during the next two years. Harvard College donated three hundred dollars. One of the grounds for giving which was urged in the appeal was the fact that Episcopal students comprised one seventh of each class at Harvard or about forty-five men in 1822, and that it was therefore essential to keep Christ Church open for their benefit. The appeal also noted that this was particularly necessary because the college authorities would not allow students the privilege of going to Boston churches, and Episcopal students were thus compelled to attend services at Holden Chapel!

[1] Batchelder, S., *ibid.*, p. 56.

About half of the fund of $3000 was used during the summer and autumn of 1825 for repairs to the exterior of the building, including a complete reshingling of the roof. Not only repairs but considerable alterations were made in the interior, including the removing of the four windows in the west wall, the two in the apse, and the two at the end of the aisles, the placing of the pulpit and reading desk inside the chancel rail, the carving of the capitals at the tops of the columns, and the conversion of the pews on the center aisle from box pews to slip pews.

The same year an instructor at Harvard who was in Orders, the Rev. George Otis, conducted the services. The parish elected him rector, but the Harvard Corporation would not allow him to accept. He continued to officiate, however, serving the church for four years, until he succumbed to typhoid fever and died in 1828 at the age of 32.

It must have been evident to the tiny congregation during "the reading period" that the parish could not possibly be revived without the services of an able clergyman. That credit may be given where credit is certainly due, this fact should be emphasized, namely, that had it not been for the considerable number of lay readers, thirteen of whose names have actually survived in the records, who officiated at the services during this period, the parish would have completely disintegrated and the building become a museum. It is noteworthy also that many of the lay readers, if not all of them, were students at Harvard University.

The church building having been thoroughly put in a state of good repair from the point of view of beauty and utility, the parish at last found a clergyman who was willing to accept the position of rector, which meant undertaking the task of attracting and building a congregation large enough to support the work of the parish.

In 1829, the Rev. Thomas W. Coit, D.D., rector of St. Peter's Church, Salem, became rector and for six years worked to make a parish in name become a parish in reality. In 1835 Dr. Coit accepted a call to Lexington, Kentucky, and the Rev. Mark Antony DeWolfe Howe, D.D., accepted the rectorship from which he was to resign ten months later for reasons of health. From 1837 to 1839 the Rev. Thomas H. Vail served as rector, but it was not until the close of 1839 that a young man willing to throw in his lot with the parish was discovered in the person of the Rev. Nicholas Hoppin, D.D.

Can the reader recall any parish which has had a more extraordinary history than that of the first eighty-four years of the existence of Christ Church parish? Could any church survive more "slings and arrows of outrageous fortune" than did this parish in those first eighty years? Christ Church owes an immeasurable debt to the lay readers and, indeed, to Harvard University from whose uncongenial religious atmosphere most of them came. Had it not been for these student lay readers, Christ Church parish might have changed its ecclesiastical clothing and, like its mother parish, King's Chapel, be today a high church Unitarian fellowship!

That many of these lay readers were men of no mean ability and of true consecration is revealed by the fact that a number of them entered the Christian ministry and that two became bishops. Theodore Dehon became the second Bishop of South Carolina and the thirteenth Bishop of the Church in the United States in 1812 and Jonathan Mayhew Wainwright became provisional Bishop of New York in 1852. Of interest also is the fact that the Rev. M. A. DeWolfe Howe, who served the parish as rector for ten months in 1835–36, became the first Bishop of Central Pennsylvania in 1871.

Temporary Ministers and Lay Readers

1790–1839

1790–1791	Rev. Joseph Warren
1791	Rev. William Montague Rev. Dr. William Walter
1791–1795	Rev. William Montague Rev. Samuel Parker Mr. John Pipon Mr. Joseph Willard, Jr.
1795–1796	Mr. William Hill
1796–1797	Mr. Theodore Dehon
1797–1805	Mr. William Jenks
1806–1807	Mr. Samuel Sewall
1807–1808	Mr. Abbott
1808–1809	Rev. Asa Eaton, D.D.
1809–1811	Mr. Loring Mr. Samuel Sewall Mr. Ralph Sanger
1811–1812	Mr. Evan Malbone Johnson
1812–1815	Mr. Walter Cranston
1815–1817	Mr. Isaac Boyle
1817–1822	Mr. Jonathan Mayhew Wainwright Mr. George Otis
1822–1824	Services discontinued
1824–1828	Rev. George Otis
1829–1835	Rev. Thomas W. Coit, D.D., Rector
1835–1836	Rev. Mark Antony DeWolfe Howe, D.D., Rector
1836–1837	Rev. Walter Clark Mr. Charles Mason
1837–1839	Rev. Thomas H. Vail, Rector
1839	Rev. Horatio Southgate Rev. George Leeds Rev. John Williams

CHAPTER V

NICHOLAS HOPPIN

1839–1874

BUILDER OF THE PARISH

WHEN WINWOOD SERJEANT fled from Cambridge in 1774 there were forty communicants, and that number was not again equalled until 1837. The church still had a Tory flavor and its liturgy was essentially that of the feared and disliked Church of England. In addition, as the little flock could offer a minister neither a living wage nor a home, their prospects of securing a permanent rector seemed almost negligible.

Fortune smiled, however, when on the first Sunday in Advent, 1839, a young clergyman named Nicholas Hoppin conducted the service. The twenty-seven-year-old clergyman was a native of Providence, Rhode Island, a graduate of Brown University and the General Theological Seminary, and had served for a year as the first Episcopal missionary in Bangor, Maine. The previous year he had married Elizabeth Parker, a granddaughter of Samuel Parker, the second Bishop of Massachusetts, and we may imagine that she approved the idea of a parish in Cambridge. Little did Nicholas Hoppin realize that first Sunday that he was embarking upon a ministry that was to continue for thirty-five years and to be not only the longest but probably the most significant ministry in the history of the parish, for as we shall see, Nicholas Hoppin came to a weak and struggling mission church and he left it one of the strongest parishes in Massachusetts.

NICHOLAS HOPPIN

Cambridge in 1839

The picture of Cambridge in 1839 is so different from the Cambridge of today that it is almost impossible for us to conceive of it. Cambridge was a town which comprised three villages; Old Cambridge, roughly the area from Harvard Square to Watertown and Arlington; Cambridgeport, roughly the section of the city in what is now Central and Kendall Squares; and East Cambridge, the section of the city from Prospect Street east to Lechmere and the Charlestown Bridge; and these villages were largely separated by marshy land impassable save for a few roads on high ground and a half dozen canals. Between the three sections there was the keenest rivalry. For example, when in 1832 the citizens of Old Cambridge, as the village in the Harvard Square area was called, refused to allow a highway to be built across the Common and insisted on its preservation as public ground, the citizens of East Cambridge fought for and secured the removal of the County Court from beside the Common to East Cambridge, where it remains to this day.

The village of Old Cambridge was separated by natural boundaries from the surrounding settlements. Beyond the Charles River on the south and west almost a mile of salt marsh lay between it and Brighton; to the north and west, Mount Auburn and Fresh Pond with neighboring swamps and clay pits separated it from Watertown and Belmont; on the north and east uninhabited and almost impassable boggy land, overgrown with woods and tangled underbrush, made communication with Somerville (then part of Charlestown and East Cambridge) extremely difficult and bald Dana Hill and swamp land along the river served as a natural boundary between Old Cambridge and Cambridgeport.

In 1842 the citizens of Old Cambridge petitioned the

General Court to be allowed to be divided from East Cambridge and Cambridgeport and be incorporated as Cambridge or as Old Cambridge. After discussions at Town Meetings for several years, the proposal was defeated and the three villages were incorporated as the City of Cambridge in 1846, with a population of about 12,000 inhabitants.

Of a Sunday, worshippers might choose, besides Christ Church, to attend the First Parish Church Unitarian; the Orthodox Congregational Church, which, under the dour leadership of Abiel Holmes, had recently seceded from the Unitarian congregation; the Old Cambridge Baptist Church; Harvard's recently built Appleton Chapel; or St. Peter's Roman Catholic Church, which opened for worship in 1849.

Christ Church in 1839

While Dr. Vail, Dr. Hoppin's predecessor, reported forty-one communicants when he resigned, some of the number left with him; thus, Dr. Hoppin started with twenty-nine communicants, although the average church attendance was about fifty, including thirteen students from the college.[1] Pews were rented at $15.00 per year and the rentals for the year ending 1839 amounted to $365.00. It was customary in those days for the pew rent to pay the rector's salary, but such a sum obviously had to be increased before Dr. Hoppin could be elected rector. In four years' time, as a result of Dr. Hoppin's labor, this amount was not only increased to $922.00 but the money was raised to buy a site and build a rectory. Meanwhile Nicholas Hoppin, finding this response on the part of the parish to his ministry most encouraging and seeing the possibilities in the future of the parish, in June, 1843 accepted his election as rector.

[1] Hoppin, N. *An Anniversary Sermon*, Nov. 26, 1860.

Material Improvement

Our story now is one of steady growth and improvement under Dr. Hoppin's leadership in all phases of the life of the parish. The old organ, most of whose stops and pipes had been stolen during the Revolutionary War, was replaced by a new one. The new rectory on Follen Street was built, paid for, and occupied. The tablets containing the Ten Commandments and the Creed which came from Trinity, Boston, were placed in the rear walls of the church where the two windows now are. The growing attendance at the services required the building of a carriage shed behind the church and started a discussion of the best methods for enlarging the church. This was to be the chief topic of Christ Church conversation for fifteen years and has served as an occasional topic ever since.

In 1854 the remaining old box pews on the side aisles were turned into "slips" and all vacant spaces were filled with seats. More seats were gained, but still more were needed. Consequently, the parish debated whether to lengthen the building, to put in galleries, or to have free pews. We get an idea of what a parish meeting was like in those days when we note that there were twenty-three people present at the meeting when the shocking idea of declaring all pews free was put to a vote. It lost by a vote of fourteen to two, with seven people abstaining from voting.

The same year a room added to the west side of the church where our parish house now stands was fitted up for the Sunday School. But more seats were still needed in the church and the parish debated for several years whether to build a full sized stone parish church down by the river "suitable to a large university city" or to enlarge the church building itself. Happily the motion on the stone church was defeated, and in the summer of 1857 the present building was cut in two and the chancel and one pillar on each side were moved back, enabling the church to be enlarged twenty-three feet in length or to the extent of two windows. East Apthorp,

THE NUMBER OF WINDOWS INCREASED FROM FIVE TO SEVEN AFTER THE CHURCH WAS LENGTHENED IN 1857

the first minister who supervised the erection of the church, had written to the Society for the Propagation of the Gospel in England that "particular care has been taken to make the structure useful and durable as well as decently elegant, and in case of future accessions to the congregation it may be easily enlarged." Now almost a century afterward "timbers were found jointed, bolts were ready to be removed, and the originally anticipated enlargement was executed according to the plan of the first architect of the building." [2] The committee on the enlargement suggested that in the near future in the in-

2 *Ibid.*, Batchelder, p. 62.

terest of better lighting a high window be cut in the chancel, or that the windows, believed to have been on either side of the altar, be restored. The necessity of this was removed, however, by the introduction of gas light in 1859 and by a gift by Mr. Rufus Freeman the following year of a stained glass window for the center of the sanctuary over the altar. Samuel Batchelder points out that the outline of the Freeman window was believed to correspond closely to that of the "Venetian Window" originally designed for the place by Peter Harrison.

Although the work of enlargement only cost $2250.00, the whole community was so disastrously affected by the nation-wide panic of 1857 that the vestry minutes reveal that in order to pay the contractor it was necessary "to borrow $500.00 from Mr. George Luther Foote at great inconvenience to himself."

The Harvard Chime

While many slight alterations were made in the interior of the church the other outstanding addition of this period was the gift by a committee of Harvard undergraduates and alumni led by Richard Henry Dana, author of "Two Years before the Mast," of a chime of bells. This gift naturally raised a question that kept the congregation agitated for some time, namely, where should the bells be hung? After long consideration the parish voted to build a campanile in the rear of the church for the bells. At a meeting a month later this motion was reconsidered and defeated, however; and at a meeting about a year later (Feb., 1860) the "Trustees for the processing of the bells" were authorized to place the bells in the tower after making such alterations for strength as should be needed. Speaking of the chime in 1893, Mr. Samuel Batchelder wrote, "From the outset the bells were considered as a common object of interest and enjoyment for the whole city, and their intimate connection with the University made it an expressed part of their purpose that they should be rung, not alone on church days, but also on all festivals and special occasions of the college, a custom which is continued to the present time." The chimes were first rung on the morning of the Centennial Celebration on October 15, 1861, and as late as 1872 one of the bells was used for the city fire alarm.

The Growth of the Parish

This continuous development of the material fabric of the church is really only an outward and visible indication of an even more remarkable growth of the parish in membership and influence during the first twenty-one years of Nicholas Hoppin's ministry. The records of the Centennial Celebration in 1861 enable us to make this vivid by a few figures. Between 1839 and 1861, a period of 22 years, the population of Cambridge increased threefold, from 8000 to 26,000, but the number of communicants increased sevenfold, from 29 to 208; the number of students associated with the parish increased from 13 to 60, and the total number of people affiliated with the parish from 93 to 542; and in addition Dr. Hoppin had recently organized a Sunday School with an enrollment of 110 pupils. That Christ Church had been transformed under Nicholas Hoppin's leadership from an aided mission of the Diocese to a strong self-supporting parish is seen not only by the fact that the income from pew rents had increased from $365 in 1839 to $2165 in 1860 but also that the rector's salary had increased by 1869 from the small pew rent of 1839 to $1800, a rectory, and two months vacation.

What Manner of Man?

No one can read the record of these years without realizing that without in any way detracting from the loyal
devotion of the members of the congregation the man
to whom most credit belongs for the transformation from
a struggling mission to a strong parish is Nicholas Hoppin.
It was he that won to the parish all but a handful of its
loyal parishioners. Consequently, we find ourselves
asking: What kind of a man was Nicholas Hoppin and
what special qualities enabled him to build this parish?
The answer is that he was a man of the highest Christian
character and a superb pastor in his devotion to the
church and in his faithful ministry to his flock. He was
a quiet scholarly type of man, well versed in theology,
who had achieved particular competence as a student of
early church doctrine and practice. He evidently left
something to be desired in that generation as a preacher,
being in his manner of preaching, according to a contemporary, "too quiet to please the popular fancy."
Dr. F. E. Oliver, who wrote the only existing brief memoir
about him, after ascribing his singularly effective ministry to his natural ability and faithful pastoral care,
writes, "There was a sweetness in his nature, and a gentle-
ness and courtesy in his demeanor, and, more than all,
a deep sense of the responsibility attached to his sacred
calling, that gave a dignity to his every act, and won the
respect and love of the humblest within his cure." [3]
"The remembrance of his constant readiness to minister
to all needs," says a writer in the *Church Eclectic*, "and
the tender sympathy and interest with which his services
were given, will long be cherished, not least by the poorer
members of his flock, who, after he had ceased to hold any
definite cure, would frequently turn to him in times of
distress and sorrow."

[3] Oliver, F. E. *Memoir of the Rev. Nicholas Hoppin, D.D.*, p. 8.

The Last Act

This chapter would have a happier ending had Dr. Hoppin's ministry closed with the Centennial Celebration in 1861, but the fact is that he continued to serve the parish for another thirteen years. During the first half of this period the parish continued to go forward. The number of communicants increased from 208 in 1861 to 260 in 1876, and the number of pupils in the church school increased in the same period from 110 to 174. The general progress of the church is further indicated by the fact that in 1862 Dr. Hoppin was elected a deputy to the General Convention; six years later a Sunday School room with a seating capacity of 150 people was erected adjoining the church; and the following year the rector was given a large increase in salary.

One of the serious problems which faces almost every minister at some time in his ministry concerns the length of time he should remain as rector of any congregation. While a minister does not always have the opportunity to leave a parish at the particular time when he feels it would be beneficial for the parish, for himself, or for both, nevertheless if he is convinced of the need for a change the opportunity for one can usually be secured. Evidently in 1869 as Dr. Hoppin entered the fourth decade of his ministry in the parish he was a dear old story to most of the parishioners, and to the young people no doubt he seemed, though barely in his sixties, a venerable grandfather with his bearded countenance and quiet, dignified mien.

Two events occurred at this time the effect of which was disastrous to Dr. Hoppin and extremely serious for the parish. The first was the opening of the new St. John's Memorial Chapel of the Episcopal Theological School, which resulted in the loss not only of a fourth of the communicants of the parish, but, because of the location of St. John's on the corner of Mason and Brattle Streets, of many of the more prosperous parishioners. At the close of his annual report to the Diocese for 1869 Dr. Hoppin stated:

> "The great reduction in communicants is partly due to the opening of St. John's Memorial Chapel, within the last year, a few rods from Christ Church. In the absence of regular transfer by canonical certificate the number thus lost cannot be definitely stated."

The other event was the relinquishing of compulsory church attendance on the part of the students by Harvard University. This resulted in the loss at the Sunday morning service of from 40 to 60 undergraduates who previously had attended Christ Church and sat in pews near the chancel. To have about a fifth of the congregation suddenly withdraw, particularly when they left vacant pews in so conspicuous a part of the church, was a severe blow to the morale of the parish, especially on top of the defection to St. John's.

Church attendance and the financial support of the parish declined so sharply as a result that by 1873 the vestry was forced to ask the rector to announce a special offering for the purpose of paying his own salary. In the middle of Lent in 1874 the vestry received two petitions from twenty-four ladies of the parish, among them several wives of vestrymen, in which these ladies, after affirming their appreciation and gratitude to Dr. Hoppin for his faithful labour "in season and out of season," and his "efforts" and "self-denial in behalf of the Parish," urgently requested that the vestry in view of the critical financial situation demand the rector's resignation.

The vestry voted its agreement with the petitions and requested two of their number, Messrs. Samuel Batchelder, Jr. and George Dexter, to wait upon the rector, lay the facts before him, request his resignation, and inform him that they had refrained from reading the petitions into the minutes of their meeting in order that for his sake the matter might be kept secret.

The committee waited upon the rector the next day, Saturday (what a way to help the rector prepare for Sunday!), and reported back to the vestry that "in the course of a somewhat prolonged interview they were unable to discover any disposition on the part of the Rector to coincide with their view of the present situation and future prospects of the Parish."

The following day, Sunday, the rector sent the committee a note stating that the matter would receive his most respectful attention but that he could only properly make his reply to a parish meeting. Three days later, in order to clarify his request that the matter be taken up at a parish meeting, the rector wrote the wardens and vestry a long letter, part of which merits quotation:

"My object," he wrote, ". . . was to gain time to prepare such a communication as I should wish to place upon record, and the multiplied engagements of the latter part of Lent render it a matter of some difficulty to get together the requisite facts and data. I fully appreciated the kind motive which led the Wardens and Vestry to propose having the whole transaction kept secret and unrecorded, from the supposed possibility of saving something to my feelings and reputation. A secret, however, which was already in the possession of twenty or thirty persons, for whose signatures the papers alluded to had been circulated, could be no secret long and in fact it was already known to parties outside of the Episcopal Church, before the papers had been given to the Vestry. The fact must and will, of course, be immediately known and talked of throughout this community, that *Ladies* of Christ Church had taken the initiative step to have their Rector removed. And I must say, that had it been the design to accomplish this object in such a way as to place the greatest stigma upon his professional character, to inflict the keenest pain, and fix an arrow which he will carry to his dying day, it could not have been done more effectually.

I am willing to believe, that not one of the kind hearts, who were induced to take part in such a very unusual mode of action, once thought of this and that they did, with pain to themselves, what they honestly believed for the profit of Christ Church. But now that it is done, it must not only be bruited through Cambridge, but on account of my long standing in the ministry and my somewhat conspicuous position as the Rector of a Parish near a leading University, it will undoubtedly be known and discussed, more or less, in Church circles throughout the land, with the usual exaggerations and misunderstanding when things travel far. The idea of keeping it quiet was, therefore, though well and kindly meant, perfectly illusory and this was the reason why I thought it best to have the whole correspondence go upon record, with such a statement of facts as I shall be able to make at the Easter meeting. This will not, of course, reach so far as the damaging report, that Ladies, to whom a Priest of the Church had so long and, by their own written statement, so faithfully and blamelessly ministered, were the foremost to put this indignity upon him. But, it will be better than saying nothing."

He then went on to point out that the vestry's action would almost certainly make it impossible for him to secure another position and be able to support his family and therefore before he resigned he requested a statement indicating that his resignation was not caused by any "want of faithfulness" in the discharge of his ministry, "unsoundness of teaching" or "mental or physical breakdown."

The sequel was that a statement was presented to Dr. Hoppin signed by seventy parishioners in which they affirmed their high esteem for him, their conviction that "the increasing financial embarrassment of the Church for the last two or three years, has been largely, if not wholly owing to a cause for which he is not responsible." The vestry gave him a statement exonerating him from any possible accusations of negligence, immorality, or heresy. Dr. Hoppin announced his resignation on Easter Monday 1874 and was presented by the parish with a purse of $4000.

Dr. Hoppin continued to live in Cambridge for twelve years until his death in 1886, supplying in various churches, including Christ Church, as occasion offered, and writing articles on historical subjects for church magazines, but he never again filled any permanent position. These last years were a sorry anticlimax to his years of vigorous service to the parish and it is a sad fact that the unhappy final years so eclipsed the many years of the exceptionally able leadership which he gave the parish that no memorial to him of any sort has ever been placed in the church.

As the text for his sermon on the One Hundredth Anniversary on October 15, 1861, Nicholas Hoppin chose the fourth verse of the thirty-eighth chapter of St. John's Gospel: "Other men labored, and ye are entered into their labors." As Nicholas Hoppin realized more keenly than most men how much he entered into and built upon the labors of those who had gone before him, so it can be truthfully said that all who today find in Christ Church a spiritual home enter into the labors of Nicholas Hoppin who built from a struggling mission a strong parish which owes him a debt of gratitude that it is not within its power to pay.

CHAPTER VI

WILLIAM CHAUNCEY LANGDON
1876–1878
A SQUARE PEG IN A ROUND HOLE

QUITE NATURALLY, the unusual and scarcely charitable treatment which Dr. Hoppin received was not an encouragement to other clergy to step into his shoes as rector of Christ Church. Indeed, the vestry had an exceedingly hard time finding a successor, for the parish was notified of Dr. Hoppin's resignation in March, 1874, and yet it was almost two years later, January, 1876, that a new rector appeared on the scene. The new rector, William Chauncey Langdon, was a sort of clerical rolling stone, but unlike the proverbial one had gathered considerable fascinating moss. The vestry brought him to Cambridge from the American Episcopal Church in Geneva, Switzerland.

Dr. Langdon's Early Years

William Chauncey Langdon was a Vermonter and a great-great-grandson of Eleazar Wheelock, the founder of Dartmouth College. The family moved west and William graduated from Transylvania University in Lexington, Kentucky. He started earning his living by teaching chemistry and astronomy, but after a year he became an assistant patent examiner in Washington and shortly afterward took up the practice of patent law. As

WILLIAM CHAUNCEY LANGDON

an avocation he was chiefly interested in promoting Christian unity. This led him to organize interdenominational Sunday Schools in Washington and with some other men he founded the first Y.M.C.A. in Washington, was a moving spirit in the founding of the national Y.M.C.A., and became its first General Secretary. In 1855, he represented the Y.M.C.A. at a world Y conference in Paris. This trip was a significant one in his life for he found that he liked living abroad and he also became interested in a reform movement then in progress within the Roman Catholic Church.

He returned to this country, entering the ministry of the Episcopal Church in 1858, and married Hannah Agnes Courtney of Baltimore the same year. He then went to Italy as chaplain of the United States legation and became the founder and first rector of St. Paul's Within the Walls, the American Church in Rome. After a break of three years as rector of St. John's Church, Havre de Grace, Maryland, he returned to Rome, this time as secretary of a Joint Committee of the General Convention of the Episcopal Church "charged to inquire into the religious and ecclesiastical aspects and consequences of the Italian Revolution." [1] He established Episcopal churches in Florence and Geneva. During his years abroad Dr. Langdon's chief interest, outside of the care of his invalid wife and his five children, Courtney, William, George, Florence, and Annie, was the Old Catholic movement; this was, in brief, an endeavor to restore to the Roman Church the principles and practices of the early Christian church. Dr. Langdon attended the Old Catholic Congresses, for a time edited their paper, and wrote many magazine articles and books concerning it.

We may imagine that after these eighteen years in Europe, Dr. Langdon cherished an opportunity to return

---

[1] *The National Cyclopedia of American Biography*, Vol. VIII, W. C. Langdon.

to America and, particularly because of his scholarly interests, to a well-known seat of learning such as Cambridge. It is probable that some parishioners who had traveled abroad knew Dr. Langdon, but the record states that he was recommended by the Bishop of Massachusetts, Benjamin Paddock, and by testimonial letters about his work written by four English and a French clergyman which appeared in *The Churchman* of October 2, 1875.

Dr. Langdon Comes to Cambridge

When Dr. Langdon with his slightly foreign accent, bearded countenance (in his picture he looks like a Civil War general) and his felicitous literary style came to Christ Church in January, 1876, he made such a happy impression with his first address that the vestry voted that "the Rector be unanimously requested to allow his address made on taking charge of the Parish to be placed upon our records and the Wardens and Vestry wish at this time to express the great pleasure and profit with which they have heard it." In the same month he was instituted as rector by Bishop Paddock at a well-attended service for which the music was supplied by the choir of St. Peter's Church (whose rector was master of ceremonies), and the necessary additional hymnals were loaned by the parish's daughter church, St. James', North Cambridge.

Despite this auspicious start, Dr. Langdon's rectorship was to be extremely short but not in the least sweet. Whether it was due to habits of isolation acquired in European tourist chapels where parish work was not expected, to a natural lack of interest in parish work, or to his ill health, the vestry by June was so disturbed that the rector did not attend their meetings that they voted a resolution requiring the clerk to notify the rector of all meetings, "that he may attend the same if he sees fit to do so." The resolution had the desired effect and the rector appeared with reasonable regularity after that.

Two Significant Events

Two events occurred during the first year which are notable in the life of the parish. First, the rector suggested a new plan "for collecting the revenues of the church by subscription," and after securing the opinion of the parish by circular in 1877, Mr. George Dexter and Mr. Samuel Batchelder drew up a plan by which a system of subscription and payment through weekly envelopes took the place of the old system of pew rents. (I wonder if Christ Church was by chance the first church to adopt such a regular method of systematic giving through the envelope system.) Part of the original resolution reads,

> "Resolved that from and after the first of January 1877 in lieu of the present pew rentals, a guarantee fund be instituted for the support of Christ Church, every family or person regularly attending the church being called upon to subscribe to such fund a specified sum, to be paid weekly or at other intervals in envelopes through the offertory . . . and further that the wardens be authorized to assign to every family or person wishing to attend Christ Church as regular parishioners a pew, or part of a pew according to the number of seats needed."

Thus the pews of Christ Church became free in 1877 and we may be proud that Christ Church must have been one of the pioneers in doing away with the old system still in vogue in many churches within our own memory, whereby Dives sat in the front pew and Lazarus was confined to the balcony.

Parish Record Book

Another event was the purchase, at the rector's suggestion, of a book "for keeping a catalogue of the members of the parish, communicants and non-communicants and other entries which would go to make up a general history of the parish." For years the qualifications for voting at a parish meeting were that a person be baptized, and that he be twenty-one years of age. For a period of six months he must have been an attendant at public worship in the parish and a contributor to its support as well as having signed the register. With the growth of the parish and the modern rapid movement of population, the keeping of the book and the necessary checking of the signatures before each parish meeting became almost impossible and so fell into disuse. No one knows what happened to the book, but our surmise is that because of these obvious difficulties a subsequent rector allowed the book to become conveniently lost. At any rate, when I came to the parish the signing of the book was still required for a qualified voter at the parish meeting, but no one knew where the book was nor had anyone seen it in recent years. So, in the revision of the parish by-laws in 1944, this anachronistic requirement was dropped as a qualification for voting membership in the parish meeting.

The Organ Comes Down

Another event which was under discussion through 1877 but did not take place until the following year was the moving of the organ from the balcony to the floor of the church and the presentation to the parish by Mr. Edward D. Harris of two hymn boards. Originally the choir sat in the balcony but it had already been brought down into the chancel during Dr. Hoppin's rectorship.

Clouds Begin to Gather

Meanwhile, in the summer of 1877 the rector was given three months leave of absence because of ill health. Unfortunately his health failed to improve; and in consequence the parish, having already endured the last lean years of Dr. Hoppin's rectorship, and the two leaner years without a rector, had run down to such an extent that at the Easter meeting in 1878 Dr. Langdon, only a year and three months after his arrival, offered his resignation to take effect the following November. Dr. Langdon stated, "My resignation was offered in consequence of the assurance given me at a conference of members of the old vestry that there existed in the Parish a general dissatisfaction and desire for a change in the rectorship." The parish most graciously voted not to accept Dr. Langdon's resignation and besought him to withdraw it, which he did with an expression of his deep gratitude and appreciation of their action. At the same time, in his letter acceding to the request of the parish to withdraw his resignation, he pointed out, "It seems to me under the circumstances that it is wiser and more conducive to future peace and quietness that I should forward the renewal of my resignation so soon as the providence of God shall afford me an opportunity of doing so." His letter clearly indicates a large division in the opinion of the parish on the matter. "The old vestry" was not in a mood to wait upon the providence of God, but at the next meeting a month later passed the following resolution:

"Whereas the financial exhibit of the treasurer of the Parish discovers the condition under which it is painfully evident that he cannot pay the appropriations made at the recent annual meeting, or especially that he will not be able to fulfill any pledge to supply the rector with a salary worthy of his acceptance, therefore be it resolved that the

action of our Rector in tendering his resignation at the last
Easter meeting to take effect the 1st of November was
magnanimous and wise. And, however much we might
individually be pained by the contemplation of the sever-
ance of these peculiarly sacred ties existing between Rector
and people, we feel constrained to place on record our approval of his course in so doing, as the one best calculated
to sustain that prosperity in the Parish which he has so
nobly and unselfishly expressed as being near his heart."

The resolution was passed by a vote of four to three and
one of the three, Mr. Shaler, immediately handed his
resignation to the clerk.

This declaration left Dr. Langdon, who was neither
desirous of nor probably physically up to an open fight
with the vestry, without any recourse save that of renew-
ing his resignation. This he did, requesting that it take
effect on November 1, 1878. The parting was in the
spirit of Christian charity, the vestry voting to allow the
Langdons to live in the rectory until it should be needed
for his successor and "cheerfully" accorded Dr. Langdon
the right to use the church for such special services as
baptisms, etc. Thus, after November 1, 1878, Christ
Church was in the unusual and unenviable position of having two unemployed ex-rectors living in the parish.

Exonerated

It now became evident that Dr. Langdon had been suffering from a nervous breakdown when he accepted the
rectorship of Christ Church, and he was not to recover
until sometime after his resignation. No records exist
which give the specific nature of his difficulties, but after
his resignation two members of the vestry and two of the
most loyal laymen in Christ Church's history, Mr. George
Dexter, and Mr. Francis Charles Foster, preferred
charges against Dr. Langdon before the Standing Com-

mittee of the Diocese (which with the Bishop constitutes the ecclesiastical authority of a diocese) for conduct unworthy of a clergyman, imputing to him "deceit, falsehood, and dishonesty," because of statements made at different times, beginning with a letter written in 1875 relative to his coming as rector of Christ Church. It is noteworthy that both Mr. Dexter and Mr. Foster were absent from the vestry meeting which demanded Dr. Langdon's resignation.

Whether through a natural lack of competence in domestic economy, or through the heavy expense of moving his wife and five children from Geneva to Cambridge, or because of his nervous condition, or because he couldn't make his salary of $2500 a year as rector of Christ Church cover the expenses of his family, Dr. Langdon apparently had run heavily into debt and had been rescued by these two gentlemen from the hands of his creditors. Mr. Dexter and Mr. Foster now found themselves facing the problem of having to pay the unemployed rector's debts for the sake of the reputation of the church.

Whatever the transactions were, the Standing Committee, after making a careful investigation, on a motion of Phillips Brooks exonerated Dr. Langdon, and Messrs. Dexter and Foster withdrew their charges, stating that, after reflecting on the doctor's statement of "Dr. Langdon's condition of debility and nervous prostration and temporary loss of mental powers" at the times of the questioned transactions, they were satisfied that "at the time of Dr. Langdon's entering upon the rectorship of Christ Church, and for sometime afterwards, his state of health both bodily and mental was such as fully to account for the discrepancies between his understanding and our own of the conversations and transactions with which our names are connected in the memorial to the Standing Committee." So the charges were withdrawn and in

March, 1879 the vestry passed a motion congratulating Dr. Langdon and the parish on this happy exoneration.

Deserved Happiness

I suppose the moral of this tale is: Don't call a rector sight unseen; but it would not be fair to the memory of Dr. Langdon if we closed this chapter of history without informing the reader of the fact that despite the impression one receives of Dr. Langdon from this account of his two unfortunate years at Christ Church, the record of his work both before and after this episode shows not only that he was a deeply spiritual, conscientious Christian clergyman, but also that many Christ Church parishioners recognized this. Four years after leaving Christ Church he had sufficiently recovered his health to become rector of St. James' Church, Bedford, Pennsylvania, where he enjoyed an exceedingly happy and successful ministry for some seven years.[2]

[2] For an account of Dr. Langdon's unusual labors after his retirement from the active ministry, see Appendix H.

CHAPTER VII

JAMES FIELD SPALDING

1879–1891

ON THE ROAD TO ROME

WITH TWO EX-RECTORS living in Cambridge, both of whom had been requested to resign by the parish, the vestry in 1879 had none too attractive an offer to make to any clergyman. In a short time, however, they found a clergyman in the small town of Portland, Connecticut, who, having endured a stormy seven years as rector of Trinity Church there, no doubt welcomed the suggestion of a change, and being of a quiet and studious nature, particularly welcomed the idea of moving to Cambridge.

James Field Spalding, the sixth rector of Christ Church, was raised a Congregationalist in Enfield, Connecticut, attended Williston Seminary, and graduated from Williams College in 1862. As an indication of his studious nature and natural eloquence we note that he was Moonlight orator in his freshman year, Logian orator in his junior year, and delivered the classical oration in his senior year. In addition, he was Phi Beta Kappa and remained for a year as tutor at the college and two years after graduation received an M.A. In 1864 he married Mary Hopper of Enfield and in the same year became the co-founder of the Round Hill School for Boys in Northampton, of which he was the associate principal for five years. What particularly influenced him to enter the ministry of the Episcopal Church we do not know, but in 1869 he was ordained by Bishop Williams and for

JAMES FIELD SPALDING

the next two years he spent an uneventful ministry as rector of St. John's Church, Ithaca, New York, from whence he came to Trinity Church, Portland, Connecticut. While serving the church in Portland he was largely responsible for the construction of the church, the building of which was made difficult by the panic of 1877. A recent rector of Trinity Church, the Rev. Malcolm J. Van Zandt, observed, "It was a hard and trying rectorship; there were friends and foes but at least we are grateful to Dr. Spalding for this lovely church edifice."

Mr. Spalding came to Christ Church the first Sunday in Advent, December, 1879, together with his wife and three sons, Walter, Henry, and Philip. The father and the three sons were all musical. Consequently, one of the first things that Dr. Spalding did was to organize a men and boys' choir. Mr. Spalding had a fine tenor voice, Walter played the organ, and the two younger sons sang in the choir. At the second meeting of the vestry after his arrival, Mr. Spalding was given permission to rearrange the pews in the chancel so as to accommodate the choir and directly after Easter in the spring of 1880 the music of the parish was led by what was in those days a great innovation, a men and boys' choir. It is believed that it was the second vested choir of men and boys to be established in an Episcopal Church in Massachusetts. Walter became successively the organist and choirmaster of St. Mark's School, at Emmanuel Church, Boston, and professor of music at the school of music at Harvard University. He has been a member of Christ Church all of his life, as indeed he still is today.

The Redecoration of the Church

The most notable event during Mr. Spalding's twelve years as rector was an entire redecoration of the interior of the church in the summer of 1883. It is almost im-

After the 1883 Redecoration in "All the
Colors of the Rainbow"

VIEW TOWARD GALLERY SHOWING "SMIBERT" TABLET
COVERING WINDOW

possible for us today, accustomed as we are to our simple, beautiful gray and white interior, to imagine the walls and ceilings of the entire church painted in rich dark colors. The decoration was carried out under the direction of Henry Van Brunt and Frank Hill Smith. I presume that Trinity Church, Boston, which had been completed about 1877 and was considered the last word in church architecture with its painted walls and enormous La Farge murals must have been the inspiration for the redecoration, as Trinity was the inspiration of the redecoration of so many churches at that time. The late Josephine F. Bumstead, who came to the parish in 1883 as a young girl, describes it thus: "The interior was striped horizontally with terra cotta, green, blue, all the colors of the rainbow, it seemed to us; then there were little cherubs leaning on their crossed arms looking down on us from the vaulting, and between them were large cockle shells, but the crowning glory to some of us were the three medallions in the chancel on either side of the altar in each of which was painted the head of an angel with long flowing hair; and above the sanctuary in gold Victorian lettering was painted our beloved text: 'Thine eyes shall see the King in his beauty; they shall behold the land that is very far off.' (Isaiah 33:17) There was a great deal to console us in what would now be called visual education during Mr. Spalding's dull sermons.

"The decoration also included a new pulpit given by Mrs. Williams. The panelling in most of the pews which had not already been removed gave way to uniform backs. It was all illuminated by many gas lights and the transformed interior which in its picture today looks hideous, was at the time considered very beautiful." In his annual report to the Diocese in 1883, Dr. Spalding wrote: "Through the generosity of a few parishioners, the church has been appropriately decorated during the past year, and at the same time, by the subscriptions of the people in general, it was completely refurnished, so that now the interior is one of the most beautiful to be seen in this community."

Miss Bumstead further commented that while "his sermons were dull; he was a devoted pastor and unquestionably more interested in the spiritual progress of his people than in external changes. He was a man of integrity and a scholar in many ways. We felt that he never quite trusted anyone to do anything. He did everything himself so far as possible, but there was one person in whom he had absolute faith, and it was well founded, and that was in Mrs. Huntington Saville. Under her remarkable personality we had an outstanding branch of the Girls' Friendly Society numbering upwards of fifty or sixty members." That Dr. Spalding was a hard working pastor is shown by the fact that he brought the communicant strength up to and slightly beyond the point reached at the height of Dr. Hoppin's ministry in 1867. It is only fair to add however that between 1867 and 1890 the city almost doubled its population.

In his Williams College class report, we read, "Mr. Spalding was one of those phenomenal old-fashioned, classical scholars who had thoroughly committed to memory all the Greek and Latin paradigms and laws of syntax." As one would imagine, committing to memory the laws of Latin and Greek syntax did not result in inspiring sermons, nor did Dr. Spalding's general studiousness, overseriousness, and preoccupation with theological problems give his ministry any popular appeal. Consequently, because of the uninspiring character of the services, the congregation began to decline in number to the benefit of the congregation of St. John's Chapel of the Episcopal Theological School, of which the Dean of the School served as rector. Miss Bumstead describes the situation as she remembers it thus: "The rich, the attractive, the socially gifted had attached themselves to St. John's Chapel where a charming Dean and his family, and no parish financial burdens, awaited them; indeed, the situation at times caused bitterness among the struggling members of Christ Church, a bitterness that never quite died out until 1931 when the congregation of St. John's merged with that of Christ Church."

Up the Ladder

Meanwhile, Dr. Spalding, following the path of so many of those who come into the Episcopal ministry from other Protestant churches, was steadily climbing the ladder of churchmanship. In 1886 he published a volume on "The Teaching and Influence of St. Augustine" which some contemporary commentators declared might well have been written by a Roman Catholic.

The Election of a Bishop

The next few years were externally uneventful, although, as it was to become evident, Dr. Spalding was passing through a period of deep intellectual and spiritual unrest. He was becoming more and more disturbed by what he considered to be the growing rationalism of the Church, as the new biblical and historical criticism gradually undermined older literal interpretation of scripture and doctrine. The direction of Dr. Spalding's thought did not become apparent to the congregation as a whole until April 29, 1891, when Dr. Phillips Brooks, of Trinity Church, Boston, was elected Bishop of the Diocese by a very large majority of both clergy and laity. It was learned then that the rector of Christ Church voted with a small minority that violently opposed Bishop Brooks' election.

After a diocese elects a bishop, before he can assume his

office, the Standing Committees of a majority of the dioceses must give their consent to his consecration as a bishop of the Church. Directly following the election of Bishop Brooks, Dr. Spalding joined a group in the Church who, viewing life from a narrow theological standpoint, carried on a campaign by writing letters and circulating pamphlets to prevent Dr. Brooks' securing the necessary consents of the various dioceses. This group felt that Dr. Brooks did not properly uphold what they considered to be the fundamental doctrines of the Church, such as the apostolic succession, the Virgin Birth, and the resurrection. They carried on this campaign, despite the exemplary character of Bishop Brooks and his unique position as one of the greatest Christian preachers in the English-speaking world at the time, because of the breadth of his views.

Generally speaking, both outside the Episcopal Church and among the evangelical and liberally minded people in the Church, Dr. Brooks' election met with a popular approval that has seldom if ever been equalled in the election of any bishop. It was a severe shock, therefore, to the members of Christ Church when they learned that Dr. Spalding not only voted against the election of Bishop Brooks but, as the record states, "He, with some other High Church clergymen, refused to sign the testimonials to the character of the Bishop-elect and also absented himself from the consecration service in Trinity Church." In contrast, it is interesting to note in passing that one of the Cowley Fathers, Arthur C. Hall, voted for Bishop Brooks; he was in consequence, as a measure of discipline, recalled to England by his Order. He in turn withdrew from the Order, returned to this country, and three years later became Bishop of Vermont.

Dr. Spalding's refusal to attend the consecration of Bishop Brooks on October 14, 1891, must have made evident to his parishioners generally the goal toward which his thinking was leading him. Speaking of that year, one parishioner commented, "Dr. Spalding's sermons have shown to the attentive listener manifest evidence of discontent and unrest, especially in the direction of an apparent desire for more absolute ecclesiastical authority than he could find in the Episcopal Church." Two weeks later, on the first Sunday in November, when the congregation arrived in church, they found to their surprise, instead of Dr. Spalding, that the Rev. J. I. T. Coolidge was the officiating minister. The latter read to the congregation a letter from Dr. Spalding in which the rector resigned his charge of the church to take effect December 1st for "personal and imperative reasons," which, as the letter said, "would be explained to the congregation on the last Sunday in November in my farewell address." Contemporary accounts indicate that the congregation was shocked by this unexpected and unexplained resignation but that most of them surmised he had finally made up his mind to enter the Roman Church. The regret that parishioners felt because Dr. Spalding was entering the Roman Church was offset by a sense of relief that he should voluntarily have decided to resign, and thus have spared the parish the unpleasant task of having to demand his resignation. This is ordinarily disagreeable enough, but had the vestry had to ask for the resignation of a third successive rector, this fact alone would have considerably dampened the ardor of any clergyman who might, in the future, receive a call to the parish.

Dr. Spalding's greatest difficulty was that of making decisions. He prided himself, however, on the fact that when he finally decided to go to Rome, he immediately announced his resignation and engaged another Episcopal clergyman to officiate in his place. He felt this course to be the honest one, noting in his farewell address that

"During this past month of my rectorship I have not officiated in any way anywhere, so that no one's conscience has been hurt." As a matter of fact, he could hardly have placed the parish in a more uncomfortable situation had he deliberately set out to do so! It was immediately rumored everywhere and even reported in the newspapers that the rector of Christ Church was going to Rome, but the papers were able to secure from Dr. Spalding neither a confirmation nor a denial. Finally, the *Boston Herald* announced on Thanksgiving Day that Dr. Spalding was leaving the Episcopal ministry and joining the Church of Rome.

Dr. Spalding's Farewell

What a day the last Sunday in November must have been in the history of Christ Church! The congregation knew in advance that Dr. Spalding was to deliver his farewell sermon and present the reasons for the step that he either had taken or was about to take. It is almost certain that on no Sunday in the parish's history did the congregation arrive in such a high state of excitement and indignation. The service was conducted by the Rev. Charles Arey, D.D., assisted by the Rev. Henry Parker, to a church packed to overflowing. When the time came for the sermon, Dr. Spalding rose, wearing a cassock and surplice but without a stole, and instead of ascending the pulpit, simply took his place in the chancel from which, according to the old accounts, "he read a manuscript slowly and deliberately and in a voice that could be heard in all parts of the church." Dr. Spalding began by saying:

"What first set me thinking in the direction that has resulted thus far in my giving up the Rectorship was the rationalism, the free-thinking, and the unbelieving in the Episcopal Church and the entire Anglican Communion . . . The point with me was that it was unchecked . . . I refer to scouting of the doctrine of the apostolic succession, to the so-called higher criticism of Holy Scripture, to the weakening of the doctrine of the Incarnation, to the out and out denial of the Virgin Birth and the bodily resurrection of our Lord, or the making of these truths only a matter of interpretation."

He tried to explain his relation to Phillips Brooks' election by saying,

"I wish to correct a misapprehension. It has been said by some that my reasons reached their culminations at the time of the recent Episcopal election for Bishop. This is a mistake. My action is just what it would have been had the highest churchman in the land been made Bishop. All that it did was to set me thinking, as I had been thinking before, and the only effect it has had, this most recent victory of advanced thought, is that it emphasizes my action, and my action emphasizes it."

After spending about half an hour explaining what was wrong with the Episcopal Church, he then launched into an exposition of the reasons why he had become convinced that the Roman Church was "the one true Church of Christ." As he began this latter part of his address, the congregation was startled to see a man rise in his pew near the front of the church and declare that Dr. Spalding had no right to use an Episcopal Church to proclaim and expound the doctrines of the Roman Church. The congregation recognized the speaker to be Mr. Frederick Stanhope Hill, the junior warden of the parish, whose wife was a convert from the Roman Church. At this point Mr. Francis C. Foster, the senior warden, was seen to move swiftly down the aisle and persuade Mr. Hill to be silent and allow Dr. Spalding to conclude his fifty minute address.

The announcement of Dr. Spalding's submission to Rome and the publication of his sermon in the newspapers came as an unexpected blow not only to the Episcopal Church as a whole but to the protestant churches in this area, so that on the following Sunday a barrage of sermons were preached from Episcopal as well as from other pulpits, replying to Dr. Spalding's attack on Protestantism and to his contention that the claims of the Roman Church were true.

The vestry, however, very wisely secured the services of Professor Kellner, of the Episcopal Theological School, as acting rector. Dr. Kellner was well known and well liked in the parish, as he had substituted for the rector many times in the past. He encouraged those who were disturbed by Dr. Spalding's action to remain loyal to the parish, serving as minister in charge for almost a year until September, 1892, when the new rector, the Rev. William Benjamin Basil King came to Christ Church from St. Luke's Pro-Cathedral, Nova Scotia.

Meanwhile, thick clouds of gloom settled upon the rectory. Mrs. Spalding and her three sons were grief-stricken, but they evidently could not change Dr. Spalding's mind. Perhaps it was their persuasive power that caused him a year later to recoil from the Roman Church back into the Episcopal Church. But his change of mind was only temporary, and shortly afterward he made his final submission. His family believed his conversion was due to the influence of some Anglo-Catholic and Roman Catholic friends he had come to know in Cambridge. A review of his life would seem to indicate, however, that he was a man whose nature demanded authority for his own inner sense of security and peace of mind and that his decisions to leave teaching for the ministry, and the Congregational Church for the Episcopal Church at the age of thirty in 1869, were but first steps in a pilgrimage which he was to follow to its ultimate conclusion twenty-five years later.

As he could not, because of his family, become a Roman Catholic priest, he devoted himself to teaching in Boston College and in other Roman institutions, living in Cambridge for the rest of his life. That his family had the hearty sympathy of the parish, and that Dr. Spalding himself was borne no ill-will by the parish, is indicated by the presentation of a gold vase to him and Mrs. Spalding on the occasion of their golden wedding anniversary on April 28, 1914. Dr. Spalding died in 1921 at the age of 82.

CHAPTER VIII

WILLIAM BENJAMIN BASIL KING

1892–1900

THE DECADE OF THE NINETIES

DURING THE DECADE of the nineties, Frederick Caesar deSumichrast, Professor of French at Harvard, is said to have been one of the most popular teachers in the University. As soon as Dr. Spalding resigned, Professor deSumichrast decided that the man who should be rector of Christ Church was his good friend, the youthful Dean of St. Luke's Pro-Cathedral at Halifax, Nova Scotia, the Reverend William Benjamin Basil King, and the zealous professor set to work to persuade the parish to call him. Although Professor deSumichrast was not at the time himself a member of the parish, he came to the parish meeting and spoke so eloquently on Mr. King's behalf that he was elected rector on March 9, 1892. Parenthetically, it is interesting to note that the persuasive professor joined the parish and a year later was elected to the vestry. During the rectorship of his friend, he was one of the most active and dominant influences in the parish.

Consequently, into the pulpit of Christ Church stepped this thirty-three-year-old Canadian clergyman. He was six feet tall and impressed everyone because of his large and robust physique. He charmed his hearers with his beautifully modulated English voice to such an extent that Miss Josephine Bumstead remarked: "So beautiful

WILLIAM BENJAMIN BASIL KING

was his rendition of the service that one scarcely needed a sermon." Nevertheless, he was an eloquent and persuasive preacher and possessed such a fine command of the English language that his sermons contained a distinctive literary quality. Mrs. King reports that he would compose his sermons while taking a walk Saturday afternoons, and that he entered the pulpit without a manuscript, preaching entirely from memory. This is evidently the reason why no copies of any of his sermons are to be found in the parish archives. Dr. Arthur N. Peaslee, who was one of his assistants, writes, "He was really eloquent in a formal, old-fashioned way. The ideas on which his sermons were based, however, were for the most part derived from conservative high church theology of a type even then disappearing." The Reverend Gibson Bell, rector of All Saints' Church, Wynnewood, Pennsylvania, at that time growing up in the family of the Junior Warden, recalls his sermons as "grand, short, scholarly, and to the point"; he also adds that "he was such an immense person physically that he overawed the rest of us." The older generation were especially pleased by his social charm.

His personality was a far greater asset than his preaching. All who knew him testified to his great and extraordinary kindliness and his unfailing courtesy, as well as to his absolute sincerity and his deep convictions. He possessed a penetrating spiritual insight, which was continually deepened through almost constant suffering. For, while he looked physically strong, his health was undermined by a painful disease of the thyroid gland. Owing to his illness he lost his eyelashes and eyebrows, his face became more and more drawn, and he had to wear ever thicker glasses, which destroyed the robust and handsome appearance he possessed when he came to the parish. Four years after he came as rector he was compelled to ask for the first of what was to be a series of leaves of absence. These were necessary in order that he might go abroad to receive special treatment in the hope of discovering a cure for his illness which was accompanied by steadily failing eyesight. The "cures" were of little avail and in 1900, after only eight years at Christ Church, he resigned, leaving the active ministry and devoting the rest of his life to writing.

One event in Basil King's life which caused a great flurry in the parish was his marriage a year after he came to the parish to Mrs. Esther Foote, the wealthy widow of Mr. George Luther Foote, who for many years had been an active member of the parish. Miss Bumstead wrote, "After the excitement was over, Mrs. King with her merry laugh, sense of humor, and her kindly interest in every parishioner, won all our hearts."

After retiring from the active ministry, Mr. King wrote some twenty novels and eight serious books. One of the former, *The Inner Shrine*, was a best seller in 1909. Of the serious books, two were devoted to one of his favorite topics, the sanctity of marriage; another, *The Abolishing of Death*, to spiritualism, and the best known, *The Conquest of Fear*, was in large measure an account of his own arduous and courageous struggle in the face of his illness, with its accompanying mental and spiritual as well as its physical suffering. Mr. King lived at No. 1 Berkeley Street until his death in 1928. In his memory, the large silver communion chalices which are used every Sunday were given to the parish.

The Heart of the Parish

Even though Basil King was rector for less than nine years, and in spite of the fact that during all those years he was handicapped by illness, nevertheless the sterling quality of his personality and his able preaching drew back into the fold many of the sheep who had gone astray during the upsetting rectorship of Dr. Spalding. The decade of the nineties was a period when social conventions, such as church attendance, were taken for granted. Families normally attended together and regularly. As Harvard and Radcliffe had not then expanded over the area near Christ Church at the expense of many dwelling houses, the parish was happily situated in the midst of a thriving community of homes. Consequently, after all the parish families and individuals had been assigned sittings, only fifty-seven remained available for visitors. I do not mean to infer that there was a hundred percent church attendance, but a parishioner entering the church in the nineties would have seen the loyal members worshipping Sunday after Sunday in the same pews, an observation that is not possible today in the midst of our rapidly changing congregation.

Among the devoted workers in that day were *Mr.* and Mrs. Francis Foster (*senior warden*), *Mr.* Benjamin Dyer Washburn (*junior warden* until 1898), *Mr.* and Mrs. A. D. S. Bell (*junior warden* after 1898), Mr. and Mrs. Hastings Doyle Wright, *Mr.* and Mrs. H. Stanhope Hill (*treasurer*), *Mr.* and Mrs. Huntington Saville (*clerk*), Mr. Sturgis Thorndike, and his mother, Mrs. S. Lothrop Thorndike, Mr. and Mrs. Samuel Batchelder, his mother, sister, and daughter, Mary; Mrs. Freeman J. Bumstead and two of her three daughters (daughter Ethel went to St. Peter's); Miss Mary Edgecombe Blatchford, whose name is memorialized on a small brass plate at the end of the second pew in the church; Mr. and Mrs. Thomas Newton Cook, Prof. and Mrs. Frederick Caesar deSumichrast (Mr. deS. being particularly conspicuous for his square jet-black beard and his piercing black eyes), Mrs. George Dexter and her two daughters, Miss Mary Foote, Mr. George O. Gibbs, Prof. and Mrs. James J.

Greenough, Mr. and Mrs. George W. S. Greenough, Mr. and Mrs. Oliver Whipple Huntington, Mr. Thomas A. Jagger, Prof. and Mrs. Christopher Columbus Langdell, Prof. and Mrs. Morris H. Morgan, Mr. and Mrs. George W. C. Noble, the Rev. and Mrs. Mason G. Parker, Mrs. William E. Stone, Mr. William E. Wall, Mr. and Mrs. Joseph C. Webster. This is not an exhaustive list but a partial one of that small nucleus of hard and loyal workers that kept the heart of the parish steadily beating.

The Rector's Substitutes

As the new young rector reinvigorated the life of the parish by his personality and preaching, the feeling of parish unity became ever stronger, and a number of new parish organizations came into being. Largely because the rector's continuing illness required his absence for months at a time from the parish and partly because the work of shepherding both people and organizations was steadily more demanding, Mr. King himself arranged for substitute ministers. Among the substitute ministers who rendered considerable service to the parish were the Rev. Edward E. Atkinson and the Rev. Maximilian Kellner, the latter being a member of the Episcopal Theological School Faculty. This arrangement was obviously an extremely difficult one for the parish, leaving it in continual uncertainty as to how much authority should be assumed by the vestry and how much should be assumed by the locum tenens, or the "rector pro tem.," as he was sometimes called. Thus it was that in the fall of 1897 Professor deSumichrast by cable advised the rector, who was at that time in Europe, that the parish should have a permanent assistant minister paid by the parish. (Previously Mr. King had engaged and paid his substitute.) As the vestry had difficulty in finding a clergyman willing to serve in this capacity, it was not until 1900, when the eventual resignation of the rector plus the difficulty of being left without anyone to carry on the services was foreseen, that the Rev. Arthur N. Peaslee became the first assistant minister in the parish. This was a position that amounted to that of acting rector, and he continued to hold it until shortly after the arrival of Dr. Prescott Evarts, who came to the parish as rector in December, 1900.

The Parish Activities

Also, the illness of the rector, obviously thrusting greater responsibility not only upon the vestry but upon the whole congregation, resulted in the fact that there was probably no time in the history of the parish when so much of its work was carried on by the laity. This increased lay participation and responsibility, as is always true in such instances, greatly helped to strengthen the life and work of the parish.

A printed yearbook for the year 1899 which reports eight organizations in addition to the vestry gives us a bird's-eye picture of the parish in the last year of Dr. King's rectorship. The Sunday services were: Holy Communion at 7:30, Morning Prayer, Litany and Sermon at 10:30, with a celebration of the Holy Communion following at 11:30 on the first and third Sundays of each month. Church school met at three o'clock in the afternoon and a service of Evening Prayer at five o'clock on Fridays, with many additional services in Lent and on holy days.

Sunday services were led by a paid choir of men and boys comprising fourteen sopranos, four altos, four tenors, and six basses; however, Mr. B. Franklin Young, the organist, notes that one of the tenors and three of the basses kindly volunteered their services. During the summer, six boys were retained to lead in the congregational singing. The organist evidently experienced difficulty even in those days in securing adequate talent, for he reports, "In the course of the summer I found it expedient to advertise for tenors and basses upon whom I could rely for efficient support in our coming season's work. I obtained the singers I desired, after awhile."

The report of the Woman's Auxiliary records, "Nine meetings attended by an average of twenty women, an increase of two over last year." In addition, there was a Junior Auxiliary consisting of sixteen girls between "the ages of fifteen and twenty who have a serious purpose to devote a little time each week to the study of the Church and its missionary aspect."

The Girls' Friendly Society, which had been founded by the previous rector, the Reverend Mr. Spalding, in 1887, was the most flourishing organization because of the enthusiastic and efficient leadership of Mrs. Henry M. Saville. It comprised fifty members, twelve probationers, and eight working associates, in addition to which there was a separate class for candidates and twenty-eight honorary associates.

A boys' club, called the Apthorp Club in honor of East Apthorp (evidently a forerunner of our Boy Scout Troops), whose purpose was "to foster the spirit of manliness, courtesy, friendliness and loyalty to the Church," flourished, although it was restricted to ten boys thirteen years of age or over. The boys were particularly interested in drill. The report, after acclaiming their good fortune at having Mr. Henry N. Hudson as drillmaster, declares in a note characteristic of the decade that the following rules are strictly enforced:

1. Punctuality
2. Cleanliness of clothes and shoes
3. Cleanliness of face and hands
4. Neatness of hair

The existence of the club was evidently due to the enthusiasm of its leader, Gibson Bell, son of the Junior Warden and student at Harvard College, for after his graduation the club dissolved. Mr. Bell is now rector of All Saints Church, Wynnewood, Pennsylvania.

The Altar Guild was under the able and intrepid leadership of Miss Josephine F. Bumstead, who was to serve in that capacity until 1946! The first characteristic words of her report are of interest: "The record of the Altar Guild this last year is very similar to the seven previous years of its existence. The work has gone on quietly and steadily. Two members have resigned. One member has been admitted, leaving our total number six."

The strongest organization in the parish and quite evidently the center of parish life was the Parish House Guild, which apparently corresponds to what is now the Church Service League. Its report boasts of sixty members and further states, "The great desire of the Society has always been to count every woman in the congregation a member." The annual fee was 15 cents, and Mrs. Anna Lamb Thorndike, in closing her report, says, "The work to be done by those who are able to give time and strength besides a small fee, is so varied as to give each member an opportunity to exercise her special talent or skill, and it promotes that general personal acquaintance with each other which is so valuable in a congregation. The work is quite unselfish. It aims to promote the comfort of every parishioner — man, woman or child — and above all to make possible in our beloved Christ Church such active participation in all good works, as is a sure manifestation of the true Church of the Spirit." The Guild was chiefly concerned with the building of a new parish house, of which we shall speak further later on.

Only this single sentence mentions the church school in the yearbook, "In the Sunday School there are five teachers, three librarians, and one hundred forty children."

The vestry report shows a budget for the year 1899 of $7315.28 and a missionary offering raised by the Woman's Auxiliary of $924.00, making a total of $8,239.

Various and Sundry

It is of interest to note that the Episcopal student group at Harvard University, called the St. Paul's Society, was very active during this decade, and during Lent held an annual course of sermons at the Sunday morning services. On certain Sundays during Lent the offering was given to the Society. Eight pews were still set aside for Harvard students, and President Eliot, on his own volition, raised the contribution for the same from one hundred and twenty-eight dollars to two hundred and fifty-six dollars. The parish petitioned the city to put in a brick sidewalk in front of the church, and the city also put in the historic stone marker. In 1900, after careful consideration, the vestry declined an offer to replace the communion rail with an iron and brass rail because they felt it "their duty to preserve for posterity the chancel rail that has served for so many years." Owing to both the rector's popularity and to the growth of the community, seating of the congregations on Sundays presented increased difficulty. It was decided that the system of completely free pews was not working well. Following long study and a vote by mail by the whole parish, a new plan was put into effect which was a conservative compromise between the usual rented and the less usual free pew system. Seats were assigned to anyone pledging to the church an amount decided by themselves and indicated confidentially to the treasurer, with the latter also given authority to make assignments to people unable to pledge.

A New Parish House

The outstanding event of Basil King's rectorship, and indeed of this decade, was the building of a new parish house. Mr. King had not been in the parish a year before he realized that the old Sunday School room, as it was called, which had been given by Samuel Batchelder in 1868, was totally inadequate for the growing needs of the parish. Hence, on January 23, 1893, a day made memorable because everyone had been shocked that morning by the news of the death of Phillips Brooks, he called a meeting of the women of the parish to devise means of raising a fund to build a new parish house "as would meet present wants and make larger and more efficient work possible." A committee was appointed to arrange for a fair. Its members were Mrs. S. Lothrop Thorndike, Miss J. F. Houghton, and Miss Mary Batchelder, and it became the first "Parish House Guild." The fair was held in Brattle Hall on April 18th the same year. Miss Bumstead recalls the heated controversy that winter over the question of whether it was proper for the church to sponsor a fair. The report says, "It was a large undertaking, including a dance in the evening and a printing of a really clever newspaper containing contributions from distinguished people within and without the parish."

Early the following year it was learned that a tract of land adjoining the church could be bought for fifty cents a square foot. The fund of $1250 which the women had raised was immediately given to the vestry toward this purpose, and the land was bought for $1743. The Parish House Guild held a sale each year shortly before Christmas, and all the organizations continued to raise money for the new parish house by means of entertainment and sales. Finally, in the spring of 1897, four years after

ENTRANCE TO THE PARISH HOUSE ERECTED IN 1897

THE YARD IN WHICH THE VESTRY ROOM NOW STANDS
AT THE END OF FARWELL PLACE

the first meeting, it was decided to proceed at once with the erection of the new building. This was accomplished in the summer of 1897 at a cost of $5559.

The first meeting in the new parish house was a house-warming held on October 14, 1897. How continuously the new building was used is indicated by the fact that from September through June, in 1899, four hundred and eleven meetings were held in it. Mrs. Thorndike's report says, "The house is going to be more and more used in an informal way for all sorts of purposes connected with the parish work. Especially, before and after services, little gatherings are apt to take place in the various rooms, three or four sometimes being in progress at once. . . . One great satisfaction connected with the enlarged house is the opportunity it gives us to be hospitable to our neighbors. . . . No one connected with our own parish work can fail to notice the fresh impetus it has already given to activity in many directions. Well warmed, well lighted, and much improved in ventilation, it has changed what used to be drudgery into a pleasant task."

The Fur Flies

The achievement of a new parish house produced the only dissension within the parish during Dr. King's rectorship, and the severity of it, like that of many parish rows, was out of all proportion to the significance of the subject which caused it. It might well be passed over save that it is so characteristic of the period that our picture of the parish in the decade of the nineties would hardly be complete without it. It was obvious that with the new building so near the center of the Harvard Square area, there would be a great demand by organizations both within and without the parish for the use of it. Therefore, Professor deSumichrast was made chairman of a committee of the vestry to draw up rules for the use of the parish house. Evidently Mr. deSumichrast's puritanical religious views were well known, and with his appointment as chairman, fear filled the parish that only pious religious meetings would be allowed in the new building.

During the winter of 1897 the rector was abroad for his health. Mr. deSumichrast's committee was ready to report in December, but the vestry, fearing to face the repercussions in the parish of what had already manifested itself as an extremely hot potato, postponed for several meetings consideration of Mr. deSumichrast's rules. Finally, in February, owing to a petition from the associates of the Girls' Friendly, it became necessary to deal with the matter.

The vestry, with little disagreement, voted that the use of the parish house might be granted to parishioners on the occasion of church weddings, marriages, and funerals, "provided that the rooms be not used for social purposes, such as receptions in connection therewith," and further that no organizations outside of the Episcopal Church should be allowed to use the parish house without authorization by the vestry. But the fur flew when Mr. deSumichrast moved that "dancing in any form shall not be permitted in the Parish House." The vestry first took an informal vote on the motion and divided four to four. The senior warden, Mr. Francis Foster, who was in the chair, then voted in the negative and the motion was lost. A heated discussion followed during which letters from absent vestrymen were read, as well as a petition of seven of the eight associates of the Girls' Friendly "praying the vestry not to make too stringent prohibition of amusements in the Parish House and calling attention to the fact that these amusements of games, dancing informally among themselves, and simple theatrical performances, have been especially sanctioned by Mr. King and approved by the other rectors." After prolonged discussion a motion permitting dancing when it was confined to women and girls was passed by a vote of five to three, with the chair not voting; whereupon Mr. deSumichrast offered his resignation from the vestry. Being unable to persuade Mr. deSumichrast to reconsider, the vestry accepted his resignation. The vestry felt his loss to the parish to be so great, however, that six days later the vestry met and passed the following motion: "That the vestry thinks it wise not to make any permanent rules for the use of the Parish House during the absence of the Rector," and Mr. deSumichrast was reinstated.

As one might well imagine, the rector did not share Mr. deSumichrast's views on the wickedness of dancing, and when Mr. King returned the following October he evidently was able to persuade his devoted friend to change his mind. The vestry then voted, "that the committee on the management of the Parish House be and hereby is instructed that the Vestry is in favor of permitting the Christ Church branch of the Girls' Friendly Society to have dancing in the restricted form adopted by the directing associates as heretofore, but the committee is not to sanction dancing in any form if other persons than members and associates of the Girls' Friendly Society and the Rector are present at the meetings of the branch." No wonder the rector was popular! He was the only male with whom the vestry would allow the girls to dance! Since we noted Professor deSumichrast's influence in bringing Mr. King to the parish, at this point we should add that Mr. deSumichrast transferred to another parish after Mr. King's retirement.

Christian Nobility

So far as the recorded knowledge of the parish during the decade of the nineties is concerned, nothing appears to have transpired of either an outstanding or unusual nature. The parish life was no doubt typical of the era. As one reads the meagre records which exist, one realizes that the fact which made life in Christ Church different from that in other parishes was the inspiration of the magnificent spirit of Basil King, who at the age of thirty-five began to fight what seemed a losing battle against a disease which was not only incurable and painful, but thrust over his head a Damoclean sword of threatened total blindness. His parishioners could not forget as they watched him going to and fro in the parish or listened to him preach that he was bearing a cross the weight of which might at any moment cause his collapse.

In *The Conquest of Fear* Basil King tells how his fear of the future caused such incessant worry and despondency that he at one point decided to give up completely. He then tells how on the very day he reached that decision the spirit of God reached out to him through a "man I had never before seen." Let me quote his own words:

"In the light of what my new friend told me I saw I had been too busily engaged in directing my life for myself. I was like a child who hopes to make a smoothly working machine go still more smoothly by prodding it. I couldn't leave it alone. It had not occurred to me that the course of that life was God's own business, and that if I could follow the psalmist's advice and 'commit my way unto him he would bring it to pass.'" [1]

In a word, he learned in his own experience the meaning of surrendering one's life and consecrating one's future to God without reservation. To quote again:

[1] Basil King, *The Conquest of Fear*, Doubleday, Garden City, N.Y., 1921, p. 72 f.

"This was nothing new; it was only new to me.[2] . . . I had hitherto thought of trust as a gritting of the teeth and a stiffening of the nerves to believe and endure. . . . Gradually, in the light of the experience sketched above, I came to see it as simply the knowledge that the supreme command rules everything to everyone's advantage.[3] Within forty-eight hours, with no action on my part except (the Metanoia,) the change in my point of view, all misunderstandings had been cleared away.[4] To feel that I could give up being responsible for results and devote myself to my work was in itself a relief. If I tried to 'trust in the Lord and do good' — by which I suppose is meant doing my duty to the best of my small ability — He would look after the rest. . . . I was not working on what our modern idiom neatly summarizes as 'my own' — I was His agent."[5]

Through this spiritual experience, Basil King was born again. He achieved a confidence in God that gave him victory over his suffering and made him a living witness to the power of the gospel of Christ. The light of his witness shone forth not only while he was rector, but also to all who knew him during the twenty-eight years in which he continued to live in the parish after his retirement.

[2] *Ibid.*, p. 75.
[3] Basil King, *The Conquest of Fear*, Doubleday, Garden City, N.Y., 1921, pp. 81–82.
[4] *Ibid.*, p. 80.   [5] *Ibid.*, p. 75.

CHAPTER IX

PRESCOTT EVARTS

1900–1929

TRUE SHEPHERD OF THE FLOCK

WITH THE COMING of the Rev. Prescott Evarts as rector of Christ Church in December, 1900, the parish was to enter upon a new era of harmonious growth and development. The new rector, forty-one years of age and a graduate of Harvard, had already shown how splendidly a parish could grow under his leadership. He had three qualities, consecration, the ability to work hard, and an unfailing love of people, which made him a tremendously effective servant of the Kingdom. He had done an outstanding piece of work as rector of Zion Church, Wappingers Falls, New York, and as Archdeacon of Duchess County. Mr. Evarts was the first rector of Christ Church since Dr. Hoppin whose primary interest lay in the development of the life and work of the parish. He was particularly well-equipped both in interest and ability not only to organize the work of the parish but to enable it to achieve a position of leadership in the support of the work of the Diocese and the National Church. He was an able administrator, and a born pastor whose broad sympathies endeared him to all kinds and conditions of men who had the good fortune to know him. Among his many assets was his wife, Emily, who aided him in every phase of his ministry and particularly in the

PRESCOTT EVARTS

organization and guidance of the women's work of the parish, in which her initiative and enthusiasm won her the affectionate esteem of the whole parish.

Finding that during the long illness of his predecessor, Dr. King, the parish had been incurring annual deficits, Mr. Evarts immediately inaugurated a new scheme of giving in which the needs of the parish, the church school, the Diocese, and the missionary work of the Church were all brought simultaneously to the attention of the parish. So contagious was his own enthusiasm, not to mention his example of personal generosity, that at the end of his first year in the parish Mr. Frederick Stanhope Hill, the treasurer, was able to announce a surplus for the first time in many years. Thus did Mr. Evarts lay the cornerstone for a steady growth in the parish's financial resources which were to give new strength and stability to the parish. In the year before he became rector, the parish raised $6573 for the parish and $700 for the Diocese and missionary work of the Church; by the end of his rectorship the parish's budget was $28,000 annually, of which $7500 was given to the Diocese and missionary work of the Church. Above and beyond this, the parish gave its support to many other good causes, such as the Church Pension Fund, the Near East Relief Fund, and the Japanese Relief Fund following the earthquake in 1923.

Mr. Evarts also called the attention of the parish to the need for greater endowment and was instrumental in raising the total amount of the Wardens' Funds from $35,000 to $98,000. One of Mr. Evarts' great assets was his ability not only to win the loyalty of some of the ablest men in the parish but also to inspire them to give unreservedly of their time and thought to the work of the Church. Ever since the beginning of Dr. Hoppin's ministry in 1839, Christ Church had always had an unusually large number of laymen who were devoted to the work of the parish. Some rectors, however, had not taken advantage of this fact. Consequently, many of the able laymen Mr. Evarts found on the vestry and other organizations of the parish did not realize what it meant to work for the Church until Mr. Evarts began to press them into service.

He was particularly fortunate in having a group of men who were keenly concerned to make the financial organization of the parish more efficient in respect to the canvass for funds, the most economical possible expenditure of the funds, and the increase and investment of the endowment funds. These men were F. Stanhope Hill, treasurer from 1896 to 1909, Hammond V. Hayes, treasurer from 1909 to 1916, Professor Joseph H. Beale, the only vestryman to serve through the entire twenty-nine years of Mr. Evarts' rectorship, Samuel F. Batchelder, George O. G. Coale, Huntington Saville, Sturgis H. Thorndike, A. D. S. Bell, and his son, Stoughton Bell. As a result of the work largely initiated by these men, the parish led the Diocese and indeed the National Church in modernizing the methods of financing the work of a parish. In 1909, under the guidance of the Finance Committee, Christ Church became the first parish in the Diocese, if not in the country, to conduct an every member canvass and to use duplex envelopes in the raising of its funds. In the same year, Mr. H. V. Hayes became treasurer, and in accordance with the statement of Mr. Stoughton Bell, "he (Mr. Hayes) immediately put the Parish financial books on such a businesslike basis that they later became the model for the Diocese." In addition, in order to give greater emphasis to the missionary work of the Church, a separate missionary treasurership was created which continued to serve until 1943, when the missionary giving was on such a firm foundation that it was possible and more convenient to combine all the financial transactions of the parish under one treasurer.

Organizational Life of the Parish

Soon after Mr. Evarts became rector, the number of communicants passed the five hundred mark, the number of baptized persons increased to more than one thousand, and thirteen parish organizations reported at the annual meeting. The women's organizations, of which there were five, guided by Mrs. Evarts, grew by leaps and bounds.

Mr. Evarts was always cognizant of the opportunity and obligation of the parish to minister to Episcopal students at Harvard. For years the Episcopal students at the University belonged to "the St. Paul's Society of Harvard in the Parish of Christ Church, Cambridge." The Society held a reception for the new Episcopal students in the fall and held meetings every Sunday and on holy days for students throughout the academic year. As the parish grew, the religious work with students of necessity was entrusted more and more to the assistant ministers. There were a succession of these, serving the parish as a rule on two year terms. By 1921 the student work had grown to such an extent that Mr. Evarts requested that the Rev. George Lyman Paine become associate rector and devote himself exclusively to work with students. As the vestry believed the rector needed more help in the parish, they did not accede to this request; but the fact that Mr. Evarts made it indicates that he, at least, recognized the importance of student work. Two assistant ministers served the parish for more than the usual brief period, namely, the Rev. Daniel Magruder, who was assistant for six years (1915–1921), and the Rev. Cuthbert Fowler, for seven years (1923–1930).

One of the most important factors in the success of

Mr. Evarts' organizational work lay in his determination to make the church school as adequate as possible. A considerable portion of his thought and energy was devoted to it. One of his early actions on coming to the parish was to appoint a committee, whose chairman was Mr. James J. Greenough, to reorganize the school and to provide graded courses of instruction. As a result, in one year the number of pupils increased from 126 to 162 and the number of teachers from six to twenty. Christ Church led the Diocese in adopting a closely graded curriculum, and this plan was rapidly copied in many other parishes throughout and beyond the quarters of the Diocese.

Another important member of the committee which reorganized the church school was Mr. Frederick Gentleman. He was also instrumental in founding a Boys' Club which flourished for many years. This club later became one of the first Galahad Clubs to be established in the Diocese. The Galahad Club continued until 1943, at which time Troop 12 of the Boy Scouts of America, which had been started in 1933, became the chief boys' organization in the parish with the exception of the Boys' Choir.

Missionary Zeal Essential

It was the firm conviction of Mr. Evarts that the deepening of the spiritual life of the parish was directly dependent upon the zeal of its members in bringing people to acknowledge Jesus Christ as Lord and Saviour — in other words, upon the concern of the parish for the missionary work of the Church both at home and abroad. To implement this conviction he did three things. In the first place, he formed a special Missionary Society in the church with an executive council whose purpose was "to arouse interest in the missions of the Church and to foster all missionary activities of the Church," with, as we have noted before, a separate treasurer. This council continued until 1943, when its functions were combined with those of the Parish Council and the Church Service League. The Missionary Society not only stimulated a large increase in giving, but it also greatly increased the interest in missionary work on the part of the members of the parish; furthermore, it blazed the trail for the establishment of an organization of a more comprehensive scope, namely, the Church Service League.

Finding that just beyond the limits of the city of Cambridge was a rapidly growing community for whom no Episcopal Church was available, Mr. Evarts established a mission church there by procuring a vacant store and holding services in it. He then set to work to raise money to buy land and build a chapel. Thus, in 1908 St. Andrew's Church in Belmont was founded and the care of it became one of the primary duties of the assistant minister. When Mr. Evarts resigned as rector of the parish, the mission had so well developed that the Rev. Cuthbert Fowler resigned as assistant and became the first rector of the new church.

The third thing which Mr. Evarts did to implement the missionary concern of the parish was that of setting an example by giving of his own time and energy in serving the Diocese and General Church on what are often dull but necessary committees requiring considerable arduous labor. Thus, he served for twelve years on the Diocesan Board of Missions, serving as its secretary for eight years. For six years he was Examining Chaplain of the Diocese and he was also for many years secretary for the Society for the Relief of Disabled Episcopal Clergymen. For seven years he served on the Standing Committee, and as its secretary for three years. In addition he served on the Board of the Family Society, which was the chief social service agency in Cambridge, and as Chairman of the Committee on the Constitution and Canons of the Diocesan Convention, as well as once serving as a deputy to General Convention.

Needless to say, Mr. Evarts' concern for the work of the Diocese encouraged other members of the parish to offer to help. So it was that Prof. Joseph H. Beale could say at the celebration of Mr. Evarts' twenty-fifth anniversary as rector, "You have been the inspirer and guide of our activities, and you are responsible for the result as far as the activities of your parishioners are concerned. The record is rather a proud one." Prof. Beale went on to tell of the number of Christ Church members serving in virtually "every important diocesan activity." Thus Prescott Evarts laid the cornerstone for the strong support of the Diocese on the part of the parish which has continued until the present day, and which we are confident will always characterize the parish.

The Church Property

In 1910 a section was added on to the rear of the church adjoining the sacristy to afford a study and a reception room for the rector. This is the room which is now known as the vestry room plus the remainder of the section at the rear of the church building. This was a gift of Miss Blatchford and Mr. Francis C. Foster, and the plan was drawn by Charles N. Cogswell. Since the church had not been redecorated since the unfortunate Victorian decoration carried out in 1883, it was becoming more and more evident that the church needed not only thorough repainting but probably redecorating. In 1913, as a result of a study by a special committee appointed by the vestry, it was recommended that the church be covered with a roughcast or stucco in order both to save the expense of repainting and to carry out the original plans of the founders of the church. A special parish meeting was called to consider the matter. After considerable discussion the question was referred to another special committee of three persons; this committee, in turn, recom-

THE INTERIOR AFTER THE RESTORATION OF 1920

mended to a meeting held the following October that the plan be abandoned as more expensive than frequent painting. Surely we all rejoice in this decision. Owing to the outbreak of World War I the following year, all plans for the redecoration of the church were dropped until 1920. In that year one of the most important decisions of Mr. Evarts' rectorship was made, namely, to redecorate the church along colonial lines and thereby to make it look as much like the original building as practicable. It was decided to replace the brown exterior with pale gray plus a white trim, to replace the gaudy colors of the interior with simple gray and white colors, such as were in the original building, and to improve the looks of the grounds and the approaches to the church. Plans for the redecorating of the church by Mr. Clipston Sturgis were accepted and executed at a cost of $6500. In 1919, through the generosity of Miss Alberta Houghton and Mr. and Mrs. Francis S. Kershaw, electricity replaced gas light in the parish house, and the following year in the church, and the colors of the stained glass window over the altar were toned down.

Meanwhile, No. 1 Garden Street was purchased in 1916, and was designated as a memorial to Francis C. Foster, a layman who had been deeply devoted to the parish over so many years. For five years it was leased. In 1921 some $6000 was spent in remodeling it to make it convenient as a rectory for Mr. Evarts and his family. In the following year a plan for the alteration of the church grounds was carried out, including the rectifying of the surface grades, the laying of brick walks, the enlargement of the carriage drive, and the correlation of the grounds with those of the new rectory.

In 1907 a slate roof replaced the wooden shingles on the church, and in 1923 a new heating plant was installed at the cost of $6500.

Brief Mentions

The mention of a number of events during Mr. Evarts' rectorship will give further evidence of the vitality of the parish life. In 1904 the choir of Christ Church was one of two suburban choirs invited to participate in the

Church and Rectory

opening service of the General Convention in Boston. In 1911 a gala celebration was held at the one hundred and fiftieth anniversary of the opening of the church building in 1761, with addresses by Bishop William Lawrence, President A. Lawrence Lowell of Harvard, Dean George Hodges of the Episcopal Theological School, Richard H. Dana, President of the Cambridge Historical Society, Canon Norman Tucker of Toronto, Canada, and the Rev. Alexander Mann, rector of Trinity Church, Boston. As early as 1915 the progressive and ecumenical spirit of the parish was evident in the appointment of two delegates to represent Christ Church in the new federation of the seven old Cambridge churches, which has since grown into the Harvard Square Council of Churches. Furthermore, Christ Church pioneered in 1915 in being one of the first parishes in the Diocese to give the franchise to women at parish meetings. During the war, the parish house was made the center for entertaining the troops that were camped across the street on the Cambridge Common. Because of the shortage of coal, the church was unheated and services were held for a time in the parish house. In 1928, Christ Church became one of the first parishes to adopt the principle of a rotating vestry.

As we have already noted, one of Mr. Evarts' particular abilities was that of drawing into the working life of the parish many able laymen. In addition to those previously noted, mention should also be made of the following men whose devotion and hard work helped to make possible this splendid growth of the parish during Mr. Evarts' rectorship: Francis M. Babson, Henry R. Brigham, Frank M. Clark, Huntington P. Faxon, Ewing M. Hamlen, Thomas A. Jaggar, Francis S. Kershaw, Thomas W. Little, Morris H. Morgan, Clarence H. Poor, John H. Sturgis, Cushing Toppan, and William E. Wall.

Cowley Fathers

During the fall of 1923, the Society of St. John the Evangelist, known as the Cowley Fathers, an order of monks within the Protestant Episcopal Church, erected within the limits of Christ Church parish a temporary wooden building as an oratory on the banks of the Charles River. In February, 1924, the secular and religious press carried announcements that services were being held at the new oratory for "Harvard students, faculty and any other desirous of attending." The rector and vestry were naturally concerned lest this meant that the Cowley Fathers were planning to recruit a congregation and thus cause a division within the parish. In conference with the rector, a record of which was filed with the Bishop and the Standing Committee of the Diocese, Fr. Spence Burton, the superior of the order, denied any intention of establishing a congregation at the oratory in Cambridge. As a result of this understanding, a most cordial relationship was established between the parish and the order which has been happily maintained ever since. In 1936 the beautiful monastery of St. Mary and St. John replaced the small wooden oratory.

Twenty-Fifth Anniversary — 1926

On the occasion of Mr. Evarts' twenty-fifth anniversary, Dr. Basil King, who had resigned as rector owing to illness in 1900 and who was still living in Cambridge, wrote, "When I gave up the Rectorship in 1900, the Parish was still struggling to get on its feet after a series of knockdown blows which had extended back over thirty or forty years. Now it is firmly established and a great factor for good in the whole community." It was indeed true that when Mr. Evarts became rector the parish was extremely weak and was not greatly advanced beyond the point at which Dr. Nicholas Hoppin had left it. Mr. Evarts, by his great devotion and able leadership, in slightly more than a quarter of a century had made it into a great parish which participated in and affected the life of both the community and the Diocese and which gave steady support to the missionary work of the whole Church. If one were to ask the secret of Mr. Evarts' success, one would find the answer in the fact that Mr. Evarts walked with Him "in lowly paths of service free." He was a truly great pastor and cure of souls. This fact was beautifully expressed by the faculty of the Episcopal Theological School in a letter written to be read to the parish on the occasion of his twenty-fifth anniversary as rector:

"We, the members of the faculty of the Episcopal Theological School, desire to place on record our deep sense of appreciation of the services rendered to this community by the Rev. Prescott Evarts, for twenty-five years Rector of Christ Church. It is little to say that he has been a Rector; to say that he has been a faithful and loving pastor is to say that he has richly fulfilled the supreme work of the Christian ministry. He has been a devoted shepherd of his flock. The poor have turned to him for help, or rather, he has gone to them bearing loving sympathy and an understanding heart. All who know him have found in him a friend. Many to whom he has ministered in sickness and sorrow rise up and call him blessed. To young men in training for the Christian ministry he has set the inspiring example of one who walked with Christ, and who has carried the spirit of Christ into his high vocation. We wish him many more years of faithful service, and we congratulate his Parish on the long continuance of the close and sacred relationship of Pastor and People."

Merger With St. John's Chapel

In 1868 the St. John's Chapel of the Episcopal Theological School was opened for worship within a stone's throw of Christ Church. This, as we have seen, was the cause of considerable loss of both parishioners and funds to the parish (see Chapter VI). While the Dean and faculty of the Theological School conducted services on Sunday and did some pastoral visiting, the existence of a congregation in St. John's Chapel was an added burden to the members of the faculty and also caused a natural division in the life of Christ Church parish in which St. John's was located. It was a congregation which people could join who did not wish to become active in parish life. Therefore, many people in Christ Church resented it because they felt it was "a chapel of ease," with Sunday worship but without any daily work involved.

The disadvantages of having two Episcopal Churches in such close competition had long been realized by both the faculty of the Episcopal Theological School and the vestry of Christ Church. Consequently, in 1926, conversations were started between the vestry and the faculty to see if a merger of the two congregations might not be the happy solution to this problem. In April, 1929, Mr. Evarts, with characteristic vision, believing that the parish would go forward more successfully with a younger man, announced his determination to resign because of his conviction that, regardless of how hard it might be for himself and for his parishioners, "it is for the good of the Parish." The conversations between the faculty and the vestry were renewed in the hope that both congregations might participate in the choice of a new rector and have the merger an accomplished fact before his arrival. This union was effected at the Annual Meeting in January, 1930, and a month later a call was issued to the Rev. Charles Leslie Glenn to minister to the combined congregations as rector of Christ Church.

CHAPTER X

THE REV. CHARLES LESLIE GLENN

1930–1940

"A RIGHT TURN TO THE YOUTH"

IN CHOOSING the Rev. Charles Leslie Glenn as the twelfth rector of Christ Church, the parish wisely followed the advice of the Rev. Prescott Evarts and selected a young man. Mr. Glenn, who was only thirty years of age, was happily cognizant of the fact that one of the reasons for the founding of Christ Church parish was in order that its rector "by his doctrine and good example may give a right turn to the Youth who are educated there." [1] Ever since Mr. Glenn's graduation from the Virginia Theological Seminary four years earlier, he had exhibited such great enthusiasm for working with young men as well as such a marked ability in working with college students, that he had been selected by the National Council of the Church as Secretary for College Work. His reputation throughout the Church made it natural for the parish, at the gate of the Harvard Yard, to turn to him. Furthermore, he had recently married Georgiana Sibley, a young woman of great energy and organizing ability, who was fast becoming a leader in religious work with girls. It is hard to imagine the selection of a stronger team to carry on and expand the work of the parish so firmly established by Mr. Evarts and made doubly strong through the

[1] See Appendix A.

112

CHARLES LESLIE GLENN

merger that had just been effected of the congregation of St. John's Chapel with that of Christ Church.

This latter meant that to the 521 communicants in Christ Church in 1930 were added 270 communicants from St. John's, making a total of almost 800 communicants; and the number of baptized persons increased from 1000 to 1300. As St. John's Chapel ministered to the most privileged section of Cambridge, the merger gave the new rector proportionately greater resources with which to administer and develop the work of the parish.

Mr. Glenn had not been rector many months before not only the congregation but the community recognized that a leader of dynamic power had come to Christ Church. His vision of the way in which the parish should minister to people of all ages and especially to college students, his warm friendliness and his personal charm, his evident consecration to his Master, and his unique and inimitable way of presenting the gospel of Jesus Christ in his preaching produced an immediate response. A large number of people both in the city and in the University began attending Christ Church, many of whom had not previously been interested in any church.

As a consequence the parish grew rapidly in numbers, in strength and in influence. It was found necessary to have two identical morning services at 10 and 11:15 to accommodate the steadily increasing attendance on Sundays, and later a special service for students at 9 A.M. was added. The already existing parish organizations increased in vitality, and in addition many new ones sprang into being. For example, the following organizations were formed during Mr. Glenn's rectorship: the Business and Professional Women's Guild, the Junior Guild for young married women, the Young People's Fellowship for those of high school age, Boy and Girl Scout Troops, Brownies and Cubs, and in 1939 the Supper

Club for young people between the ages of 21 and 40 which in 1941 changed its name to the Fortnightly Club. As a result of this rapid increase in the number of organizations, it was found necessary to create a Parish Council to guide and co-ordinate their activities, and later an all-inclusive organization in the form of a parish Church Service League was established. In addition, Mr. Glenn was ever encouraging informal group meetings for students. It is significant to note that all except the first named of the above organizations were primarily for young people. Within five years the Church School was to reach an all-time high with an enrollment of over 350 pupils.

Quite naturally this tremendous growth in numbers and interest necessitated securing clergy to assist the rector. It was no longer possible for one assistant to do effective work if he had to divide his time between the parish and the work with students. It was evident that the parish needed an assistant minister and in addition another assistant who could devote his time entirely to student work. To provide a second assistant, however, necessitated "selling" the idea to the parish in order that the salary could be raised. Hence it was years before it was possible to have an assistant minister especially for student work. The parish was extremely fortunate, however, in the splendid series of assistants that the rector was instrumental in bringing to it. All of them were keenly interested in the work among students, although their primary work was in the parish. These assistants were: John Augustus Bryant, Robert Walcott Fay, John Cameron Grainger, Harold Bend Sedgwick, Walter Williams, H. Martin P. Davidson, Gray M. Blandy, George W. Wickersham, II, Henry Robbins, Samuel Tyler, and Francis B. Sayre, Jr.

In 1933, in order that the parishioners themselves would

be able to keep in touch with the many activities in the rapidly developing parish, the rector instituted the Christ Church weekly leaflet, which became a medium of information between himself and his parishioners.

One of the major interests of Mr. Glenn was the church school. By 1935 it had grown so large it was necessary to employ a paid secretary to administer the organization of it, and in another two years a director of religious education. Naturally, this splendid growth in the parish was reflected in the budget. During the year 1929, the last year of Mr. Evarts' rectorship, the total receipts of the parish were $28,465, of which $5126 was for capital expenses and $7523 was contributed to the Diocese and General Church. By the year 1939, the total receipts of the parish were $37,266 with $8804 being given to the Diocese and General Church.

Student Work

The most outstanding and most permanent contribution Mr. Glenn made to Christ Church parish during his rectorship was the development of the student work. As we have noted, his own interest in this work among students was a primary one. He had the gift of awakening students to interest in religion and of attracting them to the church. In the beginning of his ministry many informal groups of students had been formed. The old St. Paul's Society was superseded by the Sunday Evening Club, which in turn was to develop into the Canterbury Club in 1945.

It was essential, if the student work was to be carried on effectively, that the facilities for holding meetings be greatly increased. It was impossible to hold student meetings with any regularity in the one room parish house already overburdened with meetings of the parish organizations. Toward the end of Mr. Glenn's rectorship, the one large room was divided in two; nevertheless, it was still impossible to have two meetings with speakers conducted simultaneously in the two sections of the one room. Therefore, in 1934 Mr. Glenn persuaded the parish to purchase 19 Farwell Place with 5000 sq. ft. of land.

VIEW SHOWING THE VESTRY ROOM ADDED IN 1910 AND NUMBER 19 FARWELL PLACE BOUGHT IN 1934

This house, even with a small addition added to it, was still too small for the expanding work of the parish, so in 1935, Mr. Cushing Toppan gave the parish the house at No. 22 and 24 Farwell Place, and it was decided that this house should become the center for the student work of the parish. At the same time, Mr. Glenn persuaded the Diocese, because of the importance of more effective work for the Episcopal students attending Harvard and Radcliffe Colleges, that a special annual appropriation of $1500 be given to the parish for this work. This gift, plus $1500 secured by renting part of the new property, enabled the parish to engage a regular chaplain for students in the person of the Rev. Luther Tucker, as well as some theological students to assist him in the work, which had previously been done by the rector and his assistants in their "spare moments." Among the students who were attracted to the church to assist in the student work under Mr. Tucker's guidance was the Rev. Frederic B. Kellogg, who himself became chaplain to students in the following year, 1937. He has served in that capacity ever since, continually developing and expanding the work in a way that has more than lived up to the highest expectations of Mr. Glenn and those who founded the work.

By 1940 the student work under Mr. Kellogg's guidance was so well organized and effective that chaplains from other colleges all over the country were looking to Cambridge for guidance in the setting up of their own student work. While the relationship between the student work and the parish had always been a happy one, Mr. Glenn and the vestry felt that it would aid both the parish and the student work if the latter were incorporated separately from the parish. This would mean two things. First, that parishioners who didn't happen to be interested in the student work would realize that when they contributed to the parish their contribution was being primarily used for the furtherance of the work of the parish. And secondly, the students, parents of students, and alumni who wished to contribute to the student work, but who naturally saw no reason why they should support the local parish, could give, realizing that their contribution would be used to strengthen and extend the work in which they were most interested. Consequently, with a gift of $25,000 from Mrs. Philip Rhinelander as an initial endowment fund, the student work was incorporated under

Frederic Brainerd Kellogg

the title of the Bishop Rhinelander Foundation for College Work in memory of Philip Rhinelander. This man, as a young clergyman and as a professor in the Episcopal Theological School from 1907 to 1911, was one of the first

THE CHURCH FROM THE BURYING GROUND WITH
TOPPAN HOUSE ON THE LEFT

to see a vision of the work which the Church should be doing for college students and one of the first to try individually to fulfill that vision. Since its beginning the student work carried on by the Bishop Rhinelander Foundation under the guidance of the Rev. Frederic B. Kellogg has steadily increased in its scope and influence, and each year it has become a more vital and effective means of forwarding the Christian religion among the students at Harvard, Radcliffe, M.I.T., and the other educational institutions located in Cambridge.

The Church Property

Mr. Glenn deeply appreciated the fact that Christ
Church is not only a parish church but also an historical
landmark of great architectural beauty.   He was more
than happy, therefore, to fall in with the plans upon which

INTERIOR WITH THE NEW CHANDELIERS

the parish had already embarked beginning in 1920 to
restore the church so that it would be as far as was practicable like the original building.   By this the parish
meant that while the church building should look as
much as possible like the original building, the parish had
no intention of making the church into a museum by re-

storing the old-fashioned box pews or in any other way making it a less effective instrument for the service of the living. The committee of architects, which included Messrs. Richard Dana, Clarence H. Blackall, Roger Gilman and John Perkins Brown, gave the church unsparingly of their time and thought in insuring the fact that any changes that should be made would be in line with this general policy. For example, Mr. Francis B. Sayre offered to give chandeliers in memory of his wife, the late Jessie Woodrow Sayre. A year was taken by this committee of architects to determine the kind of material of which the chandeliers should be made and in what way they should be hung. As the result of their deliberations, the present beautiful crystal chandeliers were put in place in 1936. This same committee supervised the landscaping of the church property, giving particular attention to the lawns and to the brick walks which so greatly add to its present beauty.

During the last year of Mr. Glenn's rectorship, the present pulpit was given by Miss Mary Deane Dexter in memory of her father, Mr. George Dexter, who had been for many years an active and devoted member of the parish. The present choir stalls were given in memory of the Rev. and Mrs. Ernest Joseph Dennen by their children in 1940, and "in gratitude for the ministry of Charles Leslie Glenn," and a beautiful classical baroque organ was given by the Toppan family in memory of Sarah Moody Cushing Toppan, who had also been for many years a devoted member of the parish. The permanent baptismal font which the church had previously lacked was given by Miss Mary Batchelder.

The Old Burying Ground

Between Christ Church and the First Church Unitarian lay the Old Burying Ground which was the first free man's

burying ground. Here were buried original settlers of
1633, nine early Presidents of Harvard, soldiers of the
Revolution and of the French and Indian Wars, and many
prominent families in the commonwealth for the first
two hundred years of its history. It was owned by the
city, but unfortunately little attention had been paid to
it. The trees in it had died and it had become an unkempt
and uncared for field.

In 1933 Mr. Glenn was instrumental in helping to form
a citizen's committee to put the Old Burying Ground in a
condition of which the citizens of Cambridge might be
proud. New soil was placed over the entire surface of
the Burying Ground. A new lawn was provided, trees
were planted, and headstones were straightened. Through
the work of the Emergency Relief Agency and the Works
Progress Administration, the organizations that provided
work during the depression of the early thirties, plus contributions from public spirited individuals and patriotic
organizations, a map of the graves was made and recorded. Thus, in the public library as well as in the two
adjacent churches, information concerning the location of
the graves was made available. Once the initial work had
been done, the city agreed to keep the Burying Ground in
good condition.

Beyond the Parish

While Mr. Glenn was guiding the affairs of the parish,
his interests naturally extended far beyond the boundaries
of the parish. While working in the student division of
the National Council, he had seen the need of a society
devoted to promoting the Church's work among college
students with a freedom not possible when directly connected with the National Council. As a result, he was a
moving influence in founding the Church Society for College Work for this very purpose. He was in demand for

leadership for innumerable student conferences.   He served on the National Commission of the Forward Movement as well as on the Diocesan Departments of Youth and Religious Education.

It was therefore natural that other parishes should try to entice him away from Christ Church.   In an age of increasing mobility of population, the vestry itself realized that long rectorships such as the thirty-five years of Dr. Hoppin or the almost thirty years of Mr. Evarts were no longer likely.   Consequently, it was no great surprise, although it was the cause of great regret, when Mr. Glenn announced in the summer of 1940 that he had accepted a call to St. John's Church, Washington, D.C.

CHAPTER XI

GARDINER M. DAY

1941-

WORLD WAR II AND A NEW PARISH HOUSE

THE REV. SAMUEL TYLER, beloved senior assistant in the parish, served as acting rector from September, 1940, when Dr. Glenn left, until the arrival of the Rev. Gardiner M. Day, the thirteenth rector of the parish, on June 1, 1941. Dr. Tyler was ably assisted by the Rev. Frederic B. Kellogg, chaplain of the Bishop Rhinelander Foundation for College Work, and by the Rev. Francis B. Sayre, Jr., the assistant minister.

Mr. Day found himself in a parish marvelously vital, well organized, and teeming with activity. He quickly became aware that the great need of the parish was not for more parish organizations but rather for the strengthening of the work and the spiritual life of the existing organizations, so many of which had been initiated and rapidly developed under the inspiration of Mr. Glenn. Consequently, after Mr. Day had been rector for six months, at his first Annual Parish Meeting he told of steps which had already been taken to strengthen the work of the church school. Pre-nursery, nursery, and kindergarten departments had been added to the school. As the school had so overcrowded the facilities of 19 Farwell Place and the parish house that good teaching was extremely difficult, the addition of these new departments made it necessary to find a new home for at least part of

125

GARDINER MUMFORD DAY

the school. Through the co-operation of Dean Dun, St. John's Chapel and the classrooms of the Episcopal Theological School were made available for half of the church school.

This allowed the upper school to meet in the worshipful atmosphere of St. John's Chapel. In order that every child in the school should have the advantage not only of classroom instruction but of a service of worship in appropriate surroundings, a children's chapel was created in one of the rooms in 19 Farwell Place for the nursery and kindergarten, and another children's chapel was built in the basement of the old parish house for the first four grades. Even with these arrangements, and with the moving of the rector's office from 19 Farwell Place to the rectory, the demand for more space both for the church school and the parish organizations, not to mention the student groups, was so pressing that Mr. Day stated at the Annual Meeting that his six months had convinced him that the crying need of the parish was for a new and adequate modern parish house. He further expressed the hope that the parish would add as quickly as possible to the gift of $2000 made in 1938 by Mr. and Mrs. Arthur Musgrave as the beginning of a fund for a new parish house.

The Japanese attack on Pearl Harbor on December 7, 1941, a month before this Annual Meeting, had thrust the United States into World War II. Any thought of building a new parish house in the immediate future was out of the question, and the whole program of the parish had to be readjusted to meet the war situation. Thus, the first decade of Mr. Day's ministry naturally divided itself into two parts. During the first four years, 1941–1945, the life and work of the parish had to be planned primarily in relation to the war emergency; during the second period, 1945–1951, the great effort of the parish was centered in achieving a new and adequate parish house.

The Parish During the War

While, as one would expect, there were in the parish a few members who believed that it was wrong for a Christian to participate in war under any circumstances, the rector was supported all but unanimously when he again and again affirmed that terrible as war was, it was a lesser evil than that of refusing to aid those peoples of Europe and Asia who were fighting to preserve their freedom, and ultimately our own freedom, in the face of a ruthless and unspeakable tyranny. In one of his first sermons in June, 1941, five months before the United States' entry into the war, in interpreting the role of the Church, Mr. Day said:

"In the contest between the two opposing forces in the world today, Communism and Nazism versus the democracies, the Church has only one inescapable choice because of the obvious attempt of Communism and Nazism to destroy the freedom of man and to liquidate the Church in an effort to eradicate the beliefs for which it stands. The Church must put on the whole armor of God and stand with the democracies against these demonic forces. This does not mean that the Church gives its blessing to war. The Church will continue to decry war as one of the greatest scourges and evils growing out of the sinfulness of man. Nevertheless the Church need not bless war to recognize that war may be an evil necessary to prevent a greater evil, namely, the slavery of mankind to a godless tyranny. For in the last analysis the war is being fought to keep open the possibility of achieving a civilization governed by Christian principles."

At the same time Mr. Day further emphasized the fact that the war should be considered in a very real sense a judgment upon western civilization:

"The war is itself the result of a process of decay and disintegration that has been going on in our social and economic system for a long time. If we view western or even our own American society realistically and honestly, we must confess that our social order leaves much to be desired when measured by standards of Christian ethics or even human justice and decency. Why should we expect the unemployed, the Negro, and many other less privileged groups in our country to rise in defense of democracy? While we recognize Communism and Nazism as black, we must continue to remind ourselves that Christianity as represented by the Church and democracy as represented by our country are far from white. Therefore at the same time that the Church joins in the defense of democracy, it must never fail to attack the evil in our own social order and to challenge us to apply more realistically our Christian principles to our own social order."

He continually stressed the significance of the Church as an international fellowship of Christians and strove to make the parish a living symbol of this world-wide fellowship. He realized that the Church, outgrowing its denominational, national, and racial differences, must express its essential catholicity by making all of its members deeply conscious of their fellowship with all those in every country who acknowledge Jesus Christ as Lord and Master.

The task of the Church in wartime was twofold, its ministry to those at home, and its ministry, largely by mail, to those abroad. The work of all the parish organizations had to be redirected into channels that would aid in the war effort. Many groups, for example, rolled bandages and made surgical dressings in place of their usual activities. The entire parish engaged in a wholehearted effort to help keep up the morale of servicemen stationed in the area by providing entertainment both in homes and in the parish house. Unlimited opportunity to render this form of service was presented to the parish because Cambridge had become practically an army camp, with Harvard and M.I.T. serving as training bases for large Naval units and smaller units of the Army and Marines, including the Army Chaplains' Training School, while Radcliffe was partially taken over by the Waves.

OPEN HOUSE IN THE RECTORY LIVING ROOM
MARY DEANE DEXTER IS AT THE EXTREME LEFT

A real asset was the open house in the rectory after the Sunday morning service inaugurated by Mr. and Mrs. Day, as it presented an opportunity for servicemen, many of whom were free only on Sundays, to meet members of the parish as well as friends from other units. For example, one Sunday six servicemen from California, none of whom knew the others were in Cambridge, all met in the open house. In addition, calls came continually to the parish to help in housing families of men stationed in the area. The clergy were presented with innumerable personal problems varying from that of the soldier who, though passed by the draft board, was psychologically unfit for military service and didn't know what to do about it, to the wife who knocked on the rectory door desiring to talk to a minister because she had been driven almost hysterical by news that her husband had fallen in love with another girl and wanted a divorce. More than once the rector offered to enlist in the Chaplain's Corps, and each time the chairman of the Church's Army and Navy Commission and the ranking officers of the Army Chaplains' Training School told him that the ministry of Christ Church to servicemen in Cambridge, though not as glamorous, was of far more value in the war effort than any contribution he would be able to make as chaplain.

Unless one lived in the parish during the war period, it is hard to realize how radically war changed the life of the parish. The most drastic effect was the initial loss of manpower through the enlistment of vestrymen, church school teachers, and officers and members of organizations, some of whom had been so counted upon for their tasks that they had almost been taken for granted. The top classes were cut from the church school because boys as young as 17 years could enlist in the Navy or take industrial war jobs. Consequently the older people and the teen-agers had to pitch in and assume greater responsibility. An enormous proportion of the time of the clergy was consumed in trying to keep the parish organizations manned.

The fuel shortage and the gasoline rationing necessitated converting the heating plant from oil to coal. The church building could not be heated above 55 degrees except on Sunday. The parish house was heated comfortably only on one weekday, into which all the organizational meetings had to be telescoped. The gasoline shortage resulted in a canvass by mail replacing the traditional form of personal solicitation. This method proved so effective and so acceptable to the parish that it has been continued ever since, a canvasser calling in person only on those who fail to respond to the canvass letter. This process of eliminating all nonessential activities resulted in 1943 in the consolidation of the Missionary Council with the Parish Council and the Church Service League, while at the same time the duties of the missionary treasurer were assumed by the parish treasurer, as had been the case until 1911. In the thirty-two years of its existence the Missionary Council had performed its task of educating the parish so well that the parish's contribution to the work of the Diocese and General Church was as a rule only exceeded by that of Trinity Church, Boston.

At no point in the parish was the war manpower shortage felt more seriously than in the choir. It became so difficult to secure men's voices that the proportion of women in the choir had to be greatly increased. The parish was fortunate, however, after the resignation of William Judson Rand as organist and choir director in 1943, to secure as his successor Alfred Nash Patterson. Particularly talented as a choral director, with the additional gift of maintaining a high esprit de corps in his choir, Mr. Patterson attracted servicemen stationed in Cambridge because they enjoyed singing under his direction. He was thus able to maintain even during the war the Polyphonic Choir which after the war he was to develop so successfully until he resigned to become organist at the Church of the Advent in Boston in September, 1949. Again the parish was more than fortunate in

CHURCH, CHOIR AND CONGREGATION TAKEN AT THE
CLOSE OF A SUNDAY SERVICE

securing as his successor Miss Marion Boron, an organist and choir director of outstanding ability who in the winter of 1944 had served with special distinction as the organist for the student choir. Within a year Miss Boron had a choir of boys that was larger in size than any the parish had seen for more than a decade.

The other important field of Christ Church's war ministry was that of keeping in touch with the 305 members as well as with the many friends of the parish who were serving in the armed forces in various parts of the world.

The weekly parish leaflet, which was mailed to all servicemen, took on a new and more important ministry than ever before. The leaflet contained both news of the parish and excerpts from sermons in which the rector dealt with some of the problems raised by the war both in the realm of personal faith and in that of the Church and the international scene. In addition to writing periodic letters to those in the service, the rector encouraged members of the parish to write in order that every member of the parish in the armed forces would realize how deeply his service was appreciated at home. Similarly, Mr. Kellogg kept in touch with hundreds of students who had been associated with his work while studying in Cambridge.

It is appropriate that we should here record the names of the members of the parish who gave their lives in the service of their country.

James Thomas Aitchison
George Leverett Barker
John Jarvis Cape
John Gifford Crowley
Gordon Curtis
Ermand Richard Enos
Robert Satterlee Hurlbut
Francis Gibson Munroe, Jr.

Alfred White Paine
William Huston Sanders
James Balfour Sleigh
Gordon Taylor
Melville Wakefield Whipple
Frederick Wilder White
Robert Alan White
Charles Currie Wicker, Jr.

As during the war the rector tried to interpret the task of the Church in wartime, similarly as the war drew to a close, the rector endeavored to prepare the congregation for the difficult problems that would inevitably arise in the postwar period along the lines of readjustment and rehabilitation of returning veterans; the establishment of peace based on Christian principles; the amelioration of the race tension which had greatly increased both at home and abroad during the war; and the work of reconstruction and relief which would have to be extended not only to friendly nations but to people in countries which were formerly our enemies. He was convinced that some form of an association of nations was absolutely essential for the peace of the world and that such associations could only be established on the basis of greater mutual understanding and trust among men and nations. The rector continually affirmed the obligation of American Christians to do everything in their power to have the United States take the lead in the formation of such an association.

Mr. Day was fortunate in being aided by an exceptionally able group of assistant ministers: the Rev. Messrs. Samuel Tyler, senior assistant until his retirement in 1942 and a valued friend and counselor until his death four years later; Francis B. Sayre, Jr., 1939 to 1942; Michael Martin, 1942 to 1944; Angus Dun, Jr., 1943 to 1945; A. Royston Cochran, 1944 to 1945; John Porter, 1945 to 1947; Shunji Nishi, 1945 to 1946; John W. Ellison,

1946; Jack Leather, 1947 to 1949; Harold E. Taylor, 1949 to 1951; Edmund Knox Sherrill, 1951–; and the Rev. Pitt S. Willand of the faculty of the Episcopal Theological School, 1948 to 1951.

I wish that there were space to mention the several theological students who each year have worked in the parish and in many instances made a signal contribution to the life of the parish.

The New Parish House

Each year it had become more evident that no enlargement of the parish house or combination with No. 19 Farwell Place would provide a building adequate for the needs of the continually growing parish and student work. Therefore, in 1945 the vestry asked Mr. Charles Collens, the parish's consulting architect, to draw up plans for a parish house. Suggestions were collected from individuals and organizations. The result was a plan for a three-story building, 310,000 cubic feet in size, which it was estimated at the current rate of 50¢ per cubic foot would cost $155,000.

The raising of such an amount without decreasing its parish and missionary budget was a far greater project than the parish had ever before undertaken. Indeed, there were those who said it could not be done. The rector and vestry, realizing it was an essential tool for the ministry of Christ Church, decided the parish must raise the necessary money. The Rt. Rev. Henry Knox Sherrill, Presiding Bishop, then Bishop of the Diocese of Massachusetts, at the Annual Parish Meeting in 1945 gave his whole-hearted encouragement saying, "No church in as strategic a location as Christ Church has as poor physical equipment with which to carry on its ministry. I urge you to raise the money just as soon as possible so as to be ready to build as soon as the Government will allow it, after the end of the war."

Realizing the magnitude of the task, the vestry secured the firm of Ward, Wells and Dreshman to assist in
the raising of the money. With Mr. James Garfield, the
senior warden, in charge of the special gifts solicitation
and the Honorable Calvert Magruder, junior warden,

THE NEW PARISH HOUSE VIEWED FROM FARWELL PLACE

and Professor Erwin H. Schell, of the Massachusetts
Institute of Technology, as co-chairmen of the general
canvass, the campaign was launched and during the first
ten days in June $100,000 was raised in gifts and pledges.
A remarkable fact was that the largest individual gift
was only $7000. The $100,000 actually represented
hundreds of small gifts from members and former members and friends of the parish. The entire parish sup-

ported the drive so enthusiastically that it resulted in a stronger spirit of fellowship throughout the parish.

It proved impossible to build immediately, however, both because of the shortage of good material and the postwar inflation which caused building costs to double in a very short time. Month by month the possibility of building an adequate parish house grew steadily more remote. At this point, Mr. and Mrs. Arthur Musgrave, who had given the first $2000 in 1938, came to the rescue and gave the parish the two-story house No. 17 Farwell Place, now appropriately called Musgrave House. This dwelling adjoining the parish house property provided living quarters for two members of the staff, the assistant minister, and the organist and choir director, and thus made possible the elimination of two apartments in the proposed plans for the new parish house. At the request of the vestry, Mr. Collens completely revised the plans, eliminating one floor and further cutting the building from the original 310,000 cubic feet to 165,000. Even with this drastic reduction, in view of the rising costs, the parish faced the need for raising another $100,000.

At a special meeting held on June 7, 1948, the parish after considerable discussion accepted the recommendation of the vestry and voted to proceed on faith that the additional money would be given. The parish offices were moved into the rectory, Harvard University graciously allowed the use of Phillips Brooks House, free of charge, for the church school and other organizational meetings, the two nearest parish churches, the First Church Unitarian and the First Church in Cambridge, Congregational cordially invited the parish to make use of their buildings, and on July 10th the demolition of the old parish house and 19 Farwell Place began. On Easter, 1949, the playroom in the partially completed new building was used for the overflow congregation, and on August 14th, the new parish house was ready for use although it was still unfurnished save for the relatively small amount of available furniture which had been saved from the old parish house. Six thousand dollars was added to the four thousand which had been given for equipment by holding in the new parish house in December a mammoth two day auction of articles given by members of the parish.

As we write at the end of the second year in the new building, it is no exaggeration to state that it has more than surpassed our expectations. With space enough to do more effective work, not only did the church school enrollment jump from 215 to over 300 pupils, but the parish organizations as well as the student work increased both in numbers and in enthusiasm. Under the inspiration of a committee headed by Mrs. Henry L. Sigourney, a weekly work day, to which all members of the parish were invited, was instituted and proved signally successful.

The cost of the building and its equipment amounted to $236,000, while other expenses, including various necessary alterations and additions to the church property, valuable improvements to the organ chamber, and the replacement of the garage, brought the total cost to $270,000. The faith of the vestry was indeed justified; $245,000 was raised, necessitating a mortgage of only $25,000. The beauty and usefulness of the building bore unexpected fruit, for when Miss Mary Deane Dexter, the last surviving member of a family which had been associated with the parish for three generations, died in June, 1950, she left an unrestricted legacy of $200,000, part of which she indicated to the rector she wanted used to complete the new building. This enabled the parish to add a number of improvements originally omitted in order to keep down the cost, including the landscaping of the grounds.

No account of the building would be complete which failed to pay tribute to the conscientious and laborious work of the building committee and particularly of Messrs. James V. Eppes and J. Edmund Vincent, who worked closely with the architects on the revision of the plans and carefully watched every detail of the construction. They gave of their time without reserve. Because of their constant care, many "on the spot" changes were made, and we have a considerably better parish house as a result.

A number of memorial rooms were given in the parish house. The parish library was given by the Rev. George Lyman Paine in memory of his wife, Clara May Paine. The chapel was given by Miss Mary Batchelder in memory of her father, Samuel Batchelder, Jr., who was junior warden of the parish from 1861 to 1864, and senior warden from 1865 until the day of his death in 1888 (with the exception of six months in 1879). The auditorium was designated by the vestry as a memorial to Mary Deane Dexter. The entrance hall was given by Mr. Thomas A. Jaggar, Jr., junior warden 1901 to 1906, in memory of his father, Bishop Thomas Augustus Jaggar. The rector's office was given by Mr. Joseph Carson, Jr., in memory of his mother, Elizabeth J. Carson. The church school office was given by Mr. and Mrs. Thomas H. Sanders in memory of their son, William H. Sanders, who was killed in World War II. The choir room was given by Mrs. Forbes in memory of her late husband, Allyn Bailey Forbes, clerk of the vestry and chairman of the music committee from 1934 until his death in 1947. The nursery room was given by Mrs. George H. May, Mrs. Clarence H. Poor, Mrs. Clarence H. Poor, Jr., and Peter T. Poor in memory of Clarence Henry Poor. The kindergarten room was given by Mrs. Gring in memory of her late husband, Mr. Paul Gring, parish treasurer

THE CHURCH AND PARISH HOUSE FROM GARDEN STREET

from 1932 to 1935. A classroom was given by the Honorable and Mrs. Calvert Magruder and Mr. and Mrs. Henry DeC. Ward, Robert S. Ward, Miss Marian DeC. Ward and Mrs. Walter Haigh in memory of Mr. Robert

THE BATCHELDER MEMORIAL CHILDREN'S CHAPEL
IN THE PARISH HOUSE

DeC. Ward and Mrs. Emma Lane Ward. A classroom was given by Miss Alice Jenckes in memory of her mother, Alice Goddard Child Jenckes. The rector's secretary's office was given in memory of the Rev. Samuel Tyler, senior assistant from 1938 to 1942 and acting rector from September, 1940 to June, 1941, by his friends in the parish. The sexton's room was designated by the vestry as a memorial to Mr. Christian Hansen, sexton from 1930

to 1944. The altar in the auditorium of the parish house
was given by Mr. and Mrs. Naboth Hedin, in memory of
their daughter, Edith, who was an active member of the
parish while a student at Radcliffe College from 1939 to
1943.

THE MARY DEANE DEXTER AUDITORIUM

In addition to the $10,000 raised to equip and furnish
the new building, many gifts of furniture were received.
Among these three deserve particular mention: a large
Bokhara rug for the library, given by Miss Mary
Batchelder; a 13 foot mahogany dining room table, given
by Mr. Stoughton Bell, which stands in a useful place in
the rear of the auditorium; and a walnut desk, table, and
five chairs used by Dr. Harry A. Garfield while President

of Williams College were given by Mr. James Garfield for the rector's office.

Before turning from our summary of the material development of the parish, a few changes in the church building deserve mention. The old brass eagle lectern, appropriate to the Victorian decoration of the church, was replaced by a wooden lectern suitable in a Colonial building, given in memory of Alice Manton Morgan by the Women's Social Club and other friends.

New sanctuary stalls were given in memory of Sydney McKenna by her parents. Narrow shelves in the rear of the church replaced the movable tables and afforded much needed aisle space. Seasonal dossal curtains, two of which were made by Mrs. Henry Ware Eliot, a member of the Altar Guild, were given to replace the old rose curtain which had covered the stained glass window for a decade. A green curtain was given by the Altar Guild in memory of Josephine F. Bumstead in 1950 and a white curtain in memory of Mary Deane Dexter in 1951.

Ecumenical Concern

Amazing as was the raising of the $270,000 for the new parish house without a decrease in the regular parish giving, even more amazing is the fact that this project did not lessen the concern nor the generosity of the parish in helping to meet the severe problems of relief and rehabilitation that faced the Church at home and abroad at the close of the war. Mr. Day had been at pains to keep the parish informed of the spirit of co-operation and spiritual unity which had been steadily increasing among the Churches throughout the world. He continually stressed the obligation which rested upon Christians in America, who had suffered so slightly in the war, to bring succor to their Christian brethren in the devastated countries of Europe and Asia. Every year found distinguished clergymen from churches in many different parts of the world speaking from the pulpit of Christ Church, and thus increasing the congregation's knowledge of the Church Universal and deepening its consciousness of fellowship with other Christians.

Even before the end of the war the parish began sending clothes and food through the World Council of Churches Committee on Reconstruction and Relief to people in those countries which had been liberated from the Nazi tyranny. This was the beginning of a steady stream of clothes which after the war was to flow not only to our allies but to people in former enemy countries in both Europe and Asia. Much food and money also were sent. In 1946, when the parish was wondering whether in the face of rising building costs it could ever raise enough money to build a parish house, its gift of over $21,000 to the National Church's "Reconstruction and Advance Fund" was only exceeded in the Diocese by Trinity Church, Boston. In addition, during the years when the parish was bending every effort to raise the money for the new building, it gave over $18,000 to the Presiding Bishop's Fund for World Relief. The Honorable Calvert Magruder headed a parish committee which was instrumental in finding places for a number of Displaced Persons in the parish. In the fall of 1950, in response to urgent appeals on behalf of the Evangelical churches in Germany struggling for survival in the face of extreme poverty and communist tyranny, the parish "adopted" the Central Deaconess House of the Evangelical Church in Berlin. This "adoption" was in accordance with a plan that had been used successfully by fifty parishes in the Diocese of Western Massachusetts whereby people not only sent food, clothes, and other necessities to people in a parish in Germany, but also by personal contact and prayer brought to at least some suffering Christians encouragement and new hope.

The ecumenical concern of the parish was further expressed by the inclusion in the regular budget starting in 1943 of an annual contribution to the Federal Council of Churches of Christ in America, and in 1947 of an equal amount to the World Council of Churches. More than $800 was contributed by the parish in 1948 to the Church of South India to help it meet the serious financial situation caused by the withdrawal of the funds by the Society for the Propagation of the Gospel.

In 1945, at the request of the Roman Catholic Church, a released-time program of religious education was inaugurated in Cambridge for the children of five public school grades. Christ Church joined with the other Protestant churches in establishing the Protestant Weekday Religious Education Council. As half of the children attending the school were found to have no church affiliation, this was virtually a home missionary project for which Christ Church added $700 to its annual budget.

A parish like Christ Church goes forward only because of the active participation of a large number of faithful and loyal members. A few of those who made particularly notable contributions to the life of the parish and have entered into eternal life were: the Rev. Samuel Tyler, beloved senior associate and acting rector; Professor Joseph H. Beale, for nearly thirty years a vestryman and fourteen years a warden; Frank H. Golding, vestryman and junior warden; Susan Sedgwick Child Scoggin, dynamic head of the Tuesday Sewing Group for many years; Clarence H. Poor, vestryman and warden, and at the time of his death treasurer of the Diocese; Allyn Bailey Forbes, for fourteen years clerk of the vestry and chairman of the music committee; Huntington P. Faxon and Paul Gring, both of whom had served as treasurers of the parish; Josephine Bumstead, president of the Altar Guild for almost half a century; Mary Deane Dexter, enthusiastic and active supporter of every phase of the work of the parish.

Personal Note

I have tried to write this account of the thirteenth rectorship as objectively as I could, considering my intimate association with the rector, but I cannot close this chapter without the joy of paying tribute to and expressing my deep appreciation of some at least of those without whose help my ministry would have been both ineffective and unhappy. Mrs. Day has been an enthusiastic companion in all my work, and her mind and imagination has been a never ending source of ideas and inspiration relative to all phases of the life and work of the parish. No one could hope for finer support and encouragement or more congenial co-operation from an associate than that which I have been given by Mr. Kellogg, the chaplain of the Bishop Rhinelander Foundation, whose work is a bright star in the Christ Church parish crown. Similarly, I cannot conceive of a wiser, more conscientious, and consistently helpful senior warden than I and the parish have been fortunate enough to enjoy in James Garfield. The new parish house is due in a very large measure to his vision and effort.

The parish, and I as its rector, have been fortunate in having the same officers of the vestry with two exceptions serve throughout the decade. These officers are: James Garfield, senior warden; the Honorable Calvert Magruder, junior warden; Mr. Walcott Thompson, than whom there is no more careful parish treasurer; Mr. Norman Dill, assistant treasurer; and the clerk of the vestry, the late Allyn Forbes, whose office was assumed in 1948 by Professor Erwin H. Schell. In 1950 Mr. Dill resigned after thirteen years of service and Mr. Manning A. Williams, Jr., was elected his successor. The Church Service League of the parish has been fortunate in having extremely able leadership during this period in its presidents, who were: Mrs. Thatcher Luquer; Mrs. Richard Evarts; Mrs. Erwin H. Schell; Mrs. Chapin Bosson; Mrs. William A. Jackson; Mrs. S. Park Harman; and Mrs. Huntington P. Faxon. Of inestimable importance for all the organizations of a parish is the "ministry" of the kitchen. For many years Mrs. William Hodges, as chairman of the hospitality committee of the Church Service League, by her capable direction enabled the kitchen in the old parish house to render such service that the parish almost forgot how tiny and inconvenient it was. On entering the new parish house, the large kitchen and the two kitchenettes were placed under the able direction of a committee of which Miss Helen Hastings was chairman.

No account of the work of the parish during the past twenty years would be complete which failed to pay high tribute to the remarkable, arduous and devoted work of Miss Alice Beale as assistant director of the Altar Guild in charge of the vesting of our choirs, of which there are usually five; two parish choirs, morning, adults and boys; evening, polyphonic; two church school choirs, primary and intermediate; and the student choir.

Would that I could pay tribute by name to the vestrymen, officers of organizations, and the many devoted and relatively inconspicuous members, who have made vital contributions to the life and work of the parish, and in particular have made my ministry these last ten years at Christ Church so rich in spiritual reward and so full, even in moments of discouragement and sorrow, of that deep joy and peace that comes only through the knowledge of our oneness in Jesus Christ and the fellowship of the Holy Spirit.

In closing, I want to affirm my conviction that any man is more than fortunate to have the privilege and joy of ministering in Christ Church. It is a great parish, challenging in its possibilities and rich in its rewards, and both its location and the quality of its membership assure it of an even greater future.

A Word from the Vestry

March 24, 1951

Ten years ago today a special committee, which had spent seven months searching for just the right man to fill what was recognized as a post of unique opportunity and challenge, presented Mr. Day's name to a meeting of the parish. His unanimous election reflected the committee's enthusiasm. His devoted and outstanding leadership since assuming the rectorship two months later has more than justified the enthusiasm.

Mr. Day has notably carried on the tradition established by his predecessors of service in the name of Christ Church to the community, the Diocese and the National Church. In the community he has served on the Cambridge Community Council, the Cambridge Weekday Church School Council, the Board of the Cambridge Tuberculosis and Health Association and the Civic Unity Committee. In the Diocese he has been a member of the Diocesan Council, the Departments of Social Relations and Christian Education and the editorial board of the diocesan paper, *The Church Militant*. He is now in his second term on the Standing Committee, of which he was elected president in 1950. He was a deputy to General Convention in 1946 and 1949 and is a member of the Joint Commission on Ecumenical Relations. He has served as a director of the Massachusetts Council of Churches and as chairman of the Massachusetts Committee on Displaced Persons and as president of the Harvard Square Council of Churches. He is also chairman of the Diocesan Committee on Arrangements for General Convention in Boston in 1952.

In the national field he has served for nearly ten years on the Committee on Race Relations of the Federal Council of Churches and for several years on the Sub-Committee on Race Relations of the National Council of our Church. In the fall of 1950 he was one of the delegates appointed by the Presiding Bishop to represent the Episcopal Church at the formation of the National Council of the Churches of Christ in America and he is now serving as a member of the Executive Committee of its Division on Life and Work.

Throughout his rectorship he has been in constant demand for Lenten and other preaching both within and outside of the Diocese. He is a frequent contributor to church magazines and has published several pamphlets, particularly on the subject of church unity and the Church of South India. He is the author of two of the Forward Day by Day booklets. In 1947 the Cloister Press published a volume of his Lenten sermons entitled *Can We Believe In God?*, and in 1949 Morehouse-Gorham published *Old Wine In New Bottles*, in which he presents a modern interpretation of the Ten Commandments.

Although for several years on Anniversary Sunday Mr. Day's sermons have dealt with some episode in the earlier life of the parish, the vestry had no inkling of his purpose to compile a complete history until the work was practically finished. He recently confessed that having collected so much material he decided to devote his vacation last summer to putting it all together in permanent form.

The vestry, not content merely to say "Thank you" for the time and effort thus expended "beyond the call of duty" and for the very valuable addition to the parish records, asked Mr. Day's permission to include in the volume itself this word of appreciation of one who has contributed so largely and in so many ways to the life and usefulness of the parish.

The Vestry

James Garfield,
   Senior Warden
Calvert Magruder,
   Junior Warden
Erwin H. Schell, Clerk
Walcott B. Thompson,
   Treasurer
Manning A. Williams,
   Ass't. Treasurer

Harding U. Greene
J. Edmund Vincent
Robert E. Meyer
H. S. Payson Rowe
Thatcher P. Luquer
G. d'Andelot Belin, Jr.
John Dry
H. Edward MacMahon
Edwin H. B. Pratt

Note: When the General Convention met in Boston in 1904 the Chairman of the Diocesan Committee on Arrangements was Mr. Richard H. Dana, and another member of the Parish, Mr. Stoughton Bell, was Secretary of the Hospitality Committee. Miss Alice Morgan and Miss Josephine Bumstead served as Secretary and Treasurer respectively of the Committee on Arrangements for the Triennial Meeting of the Woman's Auxiliary held at the same time.

CHAPTER XII

THE COMMUNION OF SAINTS

WHEN A PARISH elects a rector in the Episcopal Church, by Canon Law he is given complete authority over the worship of the church and the use of the church buildings. Hence, he may behave in his parish like a king in the days when kings were dictators, or he may guide his parish by methods that make it a vital democratic fellowship. In any case, the life of a parish is bound to reflect, as we have clearly seen, the vision, interest and quality of leadership of its rector — or sometimes, unfortunately, his lack of them. In the story of Christ Church we have observed how splendidly the parish went from strength to strength under the able leadership of Dr. Hoppin and Mr. Evarts and how, on the other hand, it suffered through the want of vital leadership under Dr. Langdon and Dr. Spalding.

At the same time, no parish can go forward without the wholehearted support of lay men and women. Every rector knows that it is the small group of consecrated and devoted souls that compose the true heart of the parish. They are the saints, who, thank God, are found in every parish in every generation. They do the laborious routine work that must be done day in and day out if the more conspicuous ministry of worship and service is to be successfully carried on. So it is to them that the rector turns when the parish faces a great task or a serious emergency, knowing that he can count upon them to meet

THE CHURCH TODAY

the challenge. They are often forgotten men and women. Many of them never hold office. Their names are not recorded for posterity and yet God knows that they were "choice vessels of His grace and the light of the world in their several generations."

Christ Church has been extremely fortunate in the large number of devoted lay men and women who have been enthusiastic and valued members of the parish. Would that it were possible to tell the story of all of them and of their countless contributions to the parish, but that story can never be written, because the records are too scanty, and because the chief records of the parish, the minutes of the vestry and annual meetings, give an account of the financial and material changes in the parish, but tell little of its spiritual development. The saints who become parish officers are recorded, but the saints who never hold office but in other ways make unique contributions to the life of the parish are not mentioned.

For example, who would deny that the credit for the major portion of the work of most parishes is due to the women. Dr. Hoppin knew, to his sorrow, who really ran the parish when a group of women pushed the vestry into demanding his resignation. The vestry acquiesced, but it was the women who took the initiative and forced the issue.

Yet in the records of the stated meetings, women as a rule are only mentioned in the case of an acknowledgment of a gift, as the recipient of a letter of condolence, or as the author of a letter to the vestry. Furthermore, they held no elective offices in the parish until 1922, when Miss Mary Deane Dexter was the first woman to be elected as a delegate to represent the parish at the Archdeaconry meetings. Since then, many of our delegates to Archdeaconry Conventions have been women; and, both in 1929 and 1940, women were elected to serve on the parish committee to nominate the new rector, as well as to other important committees.

In Samuel F. Batchelder's history of the parish from 1759 to 1893, he mentioned only four women by name, one because she gave the church its first Bible, a second because she gave a silver baptismal bowl, a third because she gave an alms basin, and the fourth because in the early years of the parish's existence, she owned the pew nearest the pulpit. Only in one sentence does Mr. Batchelder mention women: "The women of the Parish, in the year 1820, subscribed and collected the sum of $420.96 as a fund toward the support of a settled minister." What is in our day a small sum represented a titanic effort on the part of the women of the parish to save its life in what Mr. Batchelder himself calls "the darkest hour of the Parish's history." The parish was so poverty stricken that it could not afford a lay reader every Sunday. Be it noted in passing that the fund given by the women was the beginning of the endowment fund, now of vital importance in the life and work of the parish.

Who can tell how much the life of the parish in its first years was dependent upon the devotion of those who bought pews when the church building was first opened. Some of their names are found in the list of officers of the parish and a few we have had occasion to mention in the narrative, but we have no way of even surmising the contribution to the parish of the others who have remained simply as names on the treasurer's books, for example, to mention but a few: Thomas Apthorp (one of the brothers of the first rector); Benjamin Faneuil (brother of Peter of Faneuil Hall fame); Brigadier-General Isaac Royall (founder of the Royall Professorship of Law in Harvard); or Madame Mehitabel Temple and her son Robert, who had the distinction of owning the small side pews closest to the pulpit.

Can we more appropriately pay tribute to such unsung members and friends of the parish in each generation than by quoting here the memorial minute of the vestry on the passing of one of i s members, Mr. William E. Wall, who had an amazing record for service to the parish on the vestry and in the choir and yet is barely mentioned in our brief history.

"William E. Wall, a Christian gentleman, passed away suddenly on Thursday, March 8, 1934. He was on his way home from the funeral of a friend at which he had been officiating.

"Throughout his life Mr. Wall was a deeply religious man. His family do not remember a day that he left his home without first reading a passage of scripture and dropping on his knees to say a prayer. As a lad, before his voice had changed, he sang in the first boy choir, and he faithfully continued ever since. He was a member of the choir of this church for 48 consecutive years, never missing a service, no matter how bad the weather, except for sickness or absence from the city. His membership on the Vestry of this church was almost as long and just as faithful.

"Mr. Wall gave unstintingly of himself to whatever he had to do, whether in his chosen field — that of a painter and grainer — and in this he stood at the head, and as such held high office, both locally and nationally — or in those evening classes for boys not so well situated as he; whether as a teacher for many years in the church school or as chairman of the property committee of the Vestry. His devotion to his duties in the latter capacity is typical of all he did. During many of the years of his chairmanship the Parish had no funds with which to make repairs. Mr. Wall made them himself. When the ball on the spire had nearly rotted away, he rebuilt it, and regilded it with gold leaf that he himself supplied. Paint he was always providing. He loved Christ Church and gave it his loving care. We loved his quiet, direct manner. We shall miss him."

The name would be different, the deeds not the same, but this minute is aptly descriptive of each of the many faithful lay men and women who have been active members of the fellowship of Christ Church Parish.

THE CHURCH BUILDING

THE ORIGINAL BUILDING was forty-five feet wide and sixty feet long. The exact height of the original tower is uncertain, but its present height is sixty-eight feet. In 1857, in order to enlarge the building, it was cut in two. The chancel and one pillar on each side were moved back, making possible an enlargement of twenty-three feet in length, providing two additional windows on each side of the church and two intercolumnar spaces. It is interesting to note that when this was done, it was found that the timbers of the church had been jointed with that intention, so that the committee ninety-eight years later was following the architect's original surmise that some day an enlargement would be needed. Oak was largely but not exclusively used in the building. The pillars were white pine felled on the upper reaches of the Charles and floated down to Cambridge. They were bored to prevent warping-cracks and then turned with machinery set up in a shop which stood until 1795 at the corner of what is now Waterhouse Street and Concord Avenue.

When it was necessary to find four new columns in 1857, the builders finally resorted to using masts of ships. These added columns may be readily recognized, for their finish is smoother than the hand hewn columns of the original building. The Ionic capitals were added in 1825. In the original building there were four windows on the west wall, one on either side of the altar on the apsal walls, and one at the end of each side aisle (on one side where the organ pipes now are, and the other side where we find the pulpit and organ console). A place was left over the altar for a painting. The treasurer's

"COME UNTO ME ALL YE THAT LABOUR AND ARE HEAVY LADEN AND I WILL GIVE YOU REST."

accounts indicate that the painting was brought from Rhode Island, but there is no record of its ever having been put in place. In 1768 a committee of the proprietors waited upon Mr. Joseph John Apthorp to thank him for his offer of an altar piece. No trace of this can be found. Mr. Apthorp was afterwards lost at sea on a passage from New York to North Carolina, and probably he was not able to fulfill his intention of giving an altar piece. The

apsal windows on either side of the altar were all eliminated in the repairs made in 1825. The central window over
the altar (now hidden by the dossal curtain) was probably
cut into the wall in 1825 as a plain window. In 1860, a
stained glass window was given by Mr. Rufus Freeman,
a devoted member of the parish at that time.

In the original building the interior walls were white
and the shutters were green. The ceilings over the aisles
and apse were flat, while that over the nave was vaulted
as it is now. The central vaulted section was painted a
chalky blue similar to that used by Peter Harrison in the
synagogue in Newport of which he was the architect.
The final form of the exterior was not roughcast but
was laid down as wide planking. The deep entablature
and cornice, much like that of the redwood library in
Newport, and the bold returned moldings over the window heads were the only external ornament that could
be afforded. The original floor extended on one level
from one end of the building to the other, the chancel
and altar platforms being added later.

The floor of the nave was divided into box pews, forty-
four in number, most of them being five feet by five feet
six inches, and all of them being of the old-fashioned,
square high-backed type. The pews were placed on either
side of the six foot center aisle. In the central bay of the
nave, on the left side of the middle aisle, was originally
the Governor's pew, occupying the entire space between
the two center columns. Records show that the pew had
the customary canopy and a parapet. The parapet was
evidently eliminated prior to the Revolution. On the
west wall was a pew twice the length of the others which
was occupied by Lieutenant Governor Thomas Oliver, a
devoted pre-Revolutionary member of the congregation.
The pews in the original building were sold to the owners,
giving way later to rented pews and eventually to free

pews. In the extensive repairs made in 1825, the box pews in the nave were changed to single rows of long slip pews, and in 1850–1855 the box pews were entirely eliminated and all available space was filled with pews similar to those we have today. It is interesting to note that in the changing of the pews as much of the wood of the original pews was used as possible. This, apparently, meant that very little new wood had to be used.

The original pulpit was a high wineglass shaped pulpit covered by a canopy. By the middle of the nineteenth century a "handsomely ornamented sounding board" had replaced the canopy. This pulpit has been replaced more than once, the present pulpit having been given by Mary Deane Dexter in 1940 in memory of Mr. and Mrs. George Dexter.

Apparently the original altar was a pine chest. Period chairs were used in the chancel until the present stalls were given in 1941 in memory of Sydney McKenna. There were no choir stalls in the nave of the church until 1880, when the first three pews on either side of the aisle were removed in order to make room for a choir of men and boys. Christ Church has the distinction of having had one of the first boys' choirs in New England. The present choir stalls were given in 1940 in memory of the Rev. and Mrs. Ernest Joseph Dennen and in gratitude for the ministry of Dr. Glenn.

In the original church building the pulpit and reading desk stood near the first column on the southerly side, in front of the chancel. The former had a sounding board above it, handsomely ornamented. In 1825 the pulpit and desk were moved within the chancel rails, the pulpit being on the south side and the desk on the north. In the Victorian redecoration in 1883 the desk was replaced by a brass eagle lectern typical of the period. This, happily, was removed in 1942 when the present desk was given by the Women's Social Club and other friends in memory of Alice Manton Morgan, who was for many years an enthusiastic member of the parish.

No one knows exactly what the original chandelier looked like but careful investigation made by Mr. John P. Brown some years ago convinced him that there was a chandelier, probably of a wooden core type with twelve wire arms, suspended from the ceiling by an iron chain. The church records indicate that the iron chain was sold for three dollars in 1859 when the oil lamps were supplanted by gas fixtures. The advent of the gas fixtures also marked the beginning of the regular evening services. Electricity replaced gas in 1918. The present beautiful crystal chandeliers were given in 1935 by Mr. Francis B. Sayre, junior warden, in memory of Jessie Woodrow Sayre.

The interior portico formed by the gallery with its balustrade, entablature, four columns and repeating pilasters is a particularly striking feature of the church. The large round-headed central door flanked by the two shorter square-headed ones distinctly add to the beauty of the church.

The back wall of the gallery is now flush with the rear wall of the church. Originally, however, when the organ was in the gallery, the organ loft extended back into the tower. The original organ was built by John Snetzler of London, England, the most eminent organ builder of his day, through the liberality of East Apthorp's brother-in-law, Barlow Trecothnick, Alderman, and later Lord Mayor of London. It was placed in the gallery of the church in 1764. This was the organ which was made famous by the fact that its pipes were melted for rifle bullets during the Revolution. It was partially restored in 1790 and replaced in 1844. A new organ was installed in 1861, another in 1883, and finally in 1940 a unique

organ of classical design typical of 18th century organ
building was given by the Toppan family in memory of
Sarah Moody Cushing Toppan.

In 1878 the organ was taken from the gallery and
placed in the chancel with the console at the head of the
right aisle near where the present organ pipes are.   In

DETAIL OF INTERIOR — SIDE AISLE AND SHUTTERS

1940 the console was removed to its present position behind the pulpit.

Originally, even before the organ had been put in place,
a fifteen hundred pound bell, the gift of Captain Edward
Cahill of London, arrived from England. The original
bell was recast in 1858, becoming the third bell in the
carillon of thirteen bells which were given primarily
through the efforts of three Harvard students, among
whom was Richard Henry Dana of *Two Years Before the*

Mast fame.[1] The present belfry, according to Dr. Nicholas Hoppin, was added in 1766. John P. Brown suggested that the belfry may not have been added until 1790. This seems unlikely, first because there are no pictures

THE PARISH LIBRARY

extant showing the church tower without the belfry, and secondly because the Diocesan Journal states that the repairs in 1790 were "slight and temporary." The addition of a belfry could hardly be considered a slight and temporary repair.

In a discussion of the tower in an unpublished manuscript entitled *One Hundred Eighty-Five Years of Christ Church*, Mr. John Sonneland writes:

[1] For a detailed description of the bells, see Appendix D.

"Mr. John P. Brown believes that (before the belfry was added) there was a balustrade around the roof of the tower, and that the balusters from the balustrade might possibly be on Judge Joseph Lee's house on Brattle Street. He also thinks that there were louvres on the lower tower and that the round windows replaced the louvres only in the repairs of 1790.

"Mr. John Brown found, in 1933, that by removing the boards and rotten beams on the east side of the tower just under the round window, he could see two dowel cuts spacing the tower in three parts, which thus proved the existence of cross beams running east and west at that level. This fact and the fact that the horizontal sheathing of the vestibule runs up to this beam shows that this was the original floor of the second stage of the tower. Mr. Brown notes that the carpenters verified the fact that the tympanum over the vestibule doors were originally part of the lower doors and all three doorways had originally arched tops. He notes that the doors originally opened inward and two iron hooks inside the main door were placed so as to hold a cross brace. . . . It is interesting to go through the belfry and notice the heavy timbers used in the early structure. We see here the early dowel joints, the mortise and tenon joints. Each tenon is held into the mortises by means of a wooden peg driven through the mortise. The same form of great, heavy beams are seen supporting the roof. Standing in the attic the forms of the truncated roof seem almost as though shaped after the ribs of a ship's hull. Perhaps a knowledge of ship construction was carried over into the form of the roof's support in 1761."

The church was unheated save for a charcoal stove placed in the vestry room, which then was the room which is now the sacristy. Three or four thicknesses of flooring boards were used in the church to protect the congregation from excessively cold feet. The present vestry room on the southern corner of the church was not added until 1910.

A water color of the church painted in 1793 by Samuel Farrar, a Harvard student, shows that the exterior of the church was gray with white trim and red doors as at present.

Letter Written by Dr. H. Caner, Rector of King's Chapel to Dr. Thomas Secker, Archbishop of Canterbury

To the most Reverend Father in God,
Thomas, Lord Archbishop of Canterbury:
Boston, New Eng., 7 April, 1759

May it please Your Grace:

Nothing less than the interest of Religion, and the advancement of that Church over which you worthily preside, could have given me the confidence of this address. With a view of promoting these good Ends, I have presumed to mention to your Grace a petition now to be laid before the Society for the Propagation of the Gospel, requesting their settling a Mission at Cambridge in New England. I should not have taken the Liberty of asking your Grace's interest in favor of it, if I did not apprehend a Mission in that place to be of great consequence to the interest of Christianity in general, as well as to that of the Church of England in particular. The College, my Lord, is placed in that town; it is the only seminary of Learning for this Province. Socinianism, Deism, and other bad principles find too much countenance among us. To prevent these and the like errors from poisoning the fountain of education, it will undoubtedly be of great service to erect a Church there, agreeable to the desire of many of the inhabitants; and to entrust the conduct of it with a gentleman, who by his doctrine and good example may give a right turn to the Youth who are educated there. Mr. Apthorp, a gentleman now in orders, and who had his Education at the University of Cambridge in England, of the same College with my Lord Bishop of Bristol, and particularly favoured by his Lordship, and who is also a Member of the Society, offers himself to this service. This gentleman appears to be every way qualified to undertake such a mission with success, and at the request of the people has promised to accept it, if the Society shall think fit to establish one in that place. They have promised a house and glebe, and £20 pr. ann., to which if the Society are pleased to add what will give Mr. A. an honourable support, I persuade myself it will be very usefully bestowed: and your Grace's influence in promoting this design will be gratefully received by that people, & humbly acknowledged by your Grace's most dutiful, &c.

                                      H. Caner

Batchelder, *ibid.*, p. 8.

Appendix B

The Prayer Used by the First Rector of Christ Church,

The Rev. East Apthorp,

on Thursday, October 15, 1761, at the Dedication of the Church

Eternal God, Parent and Sustainer of all things, Infinite in wisdom and power, justice and mercy, most humbly we adore Thy Divine Majesty, approaching Thy throne with our prayers for the Catholic Church, the whole congregation of Christians over all the earth, more especially for the reformed churches of these realms and nations.

We implore Thee, O King of kings, to crown with the blessings of heaven and earth our most Gracious Sovereign Lord, George the Third, by Thy grace King of Great Britain and Ireland and of all the dominions thereunto belonging, defender of the faith, and throughout all his realms supreme in all causes ecclesiastical and civil. Endue him with all royal virtues, prosper his arms and counsels, grant him a long and happy reign over a free and willing people, to Thy glory, the welfare of his subjects, the protection and advancement of true religion. Bless, O Lord, her Royal Highness the Princess Dowager of Wales, and all the royal family, enrich them with Thy heavenly grace, and prosper them with all happiness.

Illuminate with the truth of Thy doctrine the dispensers of Thy most holy word and sacraments, the Archbishops, Bishops, Priests, and Deacons of the Church of England and the Ministers of all other Protestant Churches. Pour down upon them the continual dew of Thy blessing, that they may be holy and exemplary in their lives and faithful stewards of Thy mysteries. Bless the nobility and magistracy, endue them with grace and wisdom, that they may all in their several characters maintain religion and virtue. In more especial duty we pray for His Excellency the Governor of this Province, His Honor the Lieutenant Governor, the Honorable Council and House of Representatives. So bless them in their respective stations, that wisdom and knowledge may be the stability of our times, and the fear of Thee our treasure.

Father of lights, from whom descendeth every good and perfect gift, grace with Thy divine favor and enlighten with Thy Spirit all seminaries of learning and religious education, particularly the Universities of England and the Colleges of this place, on whose President, Tutors, and Students we implore Thy heavenly benediction, that they may equally excell in virtue and useful knowledge.

O most gracious God, hear Thou in heaven Thy dwelling place, and behold with an eye of favor this congregation here assembled. In all humility, conscious of our own unworthiness, we implore Thy mercy, pardon and acceptance through the merits and puissant mediation of Thy Son, Jesus Christ; to whose most sacred name, and to the promoting of whose glory and kingdom we consecrate this Church, and ourselves the living temples of the Holy Ghost. Bless, we beseech Thee, all those whose pious munificence and public spirit have assisted in this good work, especially the Venerable and religious society for the Propagation of the Gospel. Grant success to their Christian purposes for the advancement of true religion, endue their ministers with fidelity to their trust, a sincere faith, unfeigned charity and sanctity of manners. Make them in their several stations the happy instruments of extending the kingdom of Thy Son, as well by supporting Thy pure worship in these colonies, as by publishing the glad tidings of the Gospel among remote and barbarous nations.

Grant, O God of truth and love, to Thy servants here before Thee, an uncorrupted, firm, and efficacious faith in the merits, mediation, and promises of their Divine Redeemer; aid and enlighten them by Thy Holy Spirit that they may sincerely practice all the duties of the Christian life, and adorn the doctrine of God our Saviour by holiness and piety, and by their ardent charity towards all mankind, especially towards all Christians of every denomination, preserving indissoluble the bond of peace and endeavoring in meekness to restore the unity of the spirit.

Finally, O God, we praise Thy holy name for all Thy servants departed this life in Thy faith and fear, beseeching Thee that we may so follow their good example, that, our probation ended, we may be partakers with them of a glorious resurrection, and of that everlasting inheritance purchased for the faithful by the most precious blood of our Lord Jesus Christ, the Saviour and Redeemer of the world; in whose prevailing intercession we trust for the acceptance, and with whose sacred words we supply all the defects of our imperfect petitions.

Our Father, &c.

Appendix C

Inscription on the Corner-stone of Christ Church Written in Latin, Samuel Batchelder's Translation Reads:

Under the guidance of the most venerable Society founded for Propagating the Gospel in Foreign Parts, the inhabitants of Cambridge, members of the Church of England, dedicated this house of worship to the Eternal God, Father, Son, and Holy Ghost, for the increase of Christian faith and charity, in the year of our Lord 1760, the Honorable Francis Bernard being governor of the province.

Batchelder, *ibid.*, p. 16.

Appendix D

The Harvard Chime

The Harvard chimes are thirteen in number, cast by Henry N. Hooper & Co. of Boston in 1859 at a cost of more than $5000. Their schedule is as follows:

No.	Pitched	Wt. Lbs.
1	D	3,100
2	E	2,100
3	F#	1,500
4	G	1,350
5	A	850
6	B	725
7	C	625
8	C#	500
9	D	450
10	D#	400
11	E	250
12	F#	200
13	G	175
	Total Weight	12,225

Each bell bears, in Latin, a portion of the Gloria in Excelsis. No. 1 also bears the inscription:

LET THE NAME OF MR. THOMAS DOWSE OF CAMBRIDGE
BE REMEMBERED
✠   THE LIBERAL MAN DEVISETH   ✠
LIBERAL THINGS

No. 2 is, as its inscription signified, in memory of the benefits of the Venerable English Society founded for Propagating

173

the Gospel in foreign parts, as a mission of which Christ Church was begun.

No. 3 is especially interesting because it is cast from the metal of the first bell possessed by the church, presented by Captain Cahill of London in 1760. It bears its original inscription, with the addition:

RECAST A.D. 1831

RECAST IN THE CHIME A.D. 1859

The chime is operated from the ringing room in the second story of the tower, where the old-fashioned system of a frame, into which the ends of the bellropes lead, is in use. The five larger bells are provided with pivots and wheels, and can be rung as well as chimed.

The chime was procured through the exertions of three Harvard graduates: R. H. Dana, Jr., class of 1837, H. M. Parker, 1839, and F. L. Batchelder, 1844, who issued a circular in 1855 proposing the idea, calling for subscriptions from all graduates and undergraduates of the college.

Batchelder, *ibid.*, pp. 79–80.

APPENDIX E

THE VASSALL TOMB

The Vassall tomb beneath the church is marked by a long, low mound in the gravel floor. This mound is the arched top of the vault, which is sunk below the surface. It is constructed of brick, with the entrance by a flight of stone steps at the western end. It was built shortly after the completion of the church by Henry Vassall, one of the original proprietors. When finally sealed in 1865 the tomb contained ten coffins, those of its owner (died 1769), his wife (1800), their only daughter, wife of Dr. Charles Russell (1802), Darby, son of Henry Vassall's negro coachman "Tony" (1861), four coffins containing the bones of children, all under two years of age (one coffin marked 1770), and one containing an unidentified man over 45 years of age. This man may have been Lieutenant Brown, one of the British prisoners of war, confined in Cambridge during the year 1778, who was shot by a sentinel for passing the lines, and "entombed in the Church at Cambridge with all military honors," according to a contemporary account. At all events, no signs of separate interments below the church have been found, though there is record of at least one such burial, that of Elizabeth Apthorp (died 1763), daughter of the first rector.

Batchelder, *ibid.*, p. 68.

Appendix F

Communion Silver

The most interesting articles of plate in the possession of
the church are the communion pieces bearing the names of
William and Mary. This set was part of a larger service presented in 1694 to the Rev. Samuel Myles, then rector of King's
Chapel, Boston, by William and Mary, the joint sovereigns
of England. It continued in use at King's Chapel until 1772.
At that date Thomas Hutchinson was appointed governor of
the province by King George III, and received from the Crown,
as was customary, communion plate and pulpit furniture to be
appropriated at his discretion. He presented this new set of
plate to King's Chapel, taking in exchange the old service, part
of which he gave to the church at Newburyport, and part to
Christ Church, Cambridge. The pieces are three in number,
a flagon, a chalice, and a paten, which forms a cover to the cup.
The flagon is 13½ inches high and of a most graceful shape; the
chalice measures 8⅜ inches in height. On the under side of the
bottom rim of each is the inscription:

THE GIFT OF K WILLIAM & Q MARY TO YE REVED
SAMLL MYLES FOR YE USE OF THEIR MAJTIES
CHAPPELL IN N: ENGLAND: 1694.

All three pieces are of thin hand-wrought silver, singularly
free from ornament, save the royal arms and the monogram
WM R which appears on each. This service is ordinarily
used only on Christmas and Easter and is kept at the Boston
Museum of Fine Arts.

In 1829 money was raised for a chalice and paten, and these

were made to match the William and Mary chalice and paten, which they do except for the inscription and coat of arms.

The Foote Memorial

In 1885 a solid gold chalice, paten, and cruet were given by Mr. Luther Foote. They were designed by Henry Vaughn and

Communion Silver and Christening Bowl

were made by Bigelow Kennard Company. The chalice is $8\frac{1}{2}$ inches high and around its stem the gold is cut in jewel-like facets.

Silver Chalices and Patens

The silver chalices and patens which are used at normal communion services were given by Dr. Basil King, the tenth rector, while the smaller intinction chalices were given, one by Mr. and Mrs. Norman Dill in memory of Robert Dill, and the other in memory of Dr. Prescott Evarts.

CHRISTENING BOWL

A silver christening basin was presented to the church in 1759 by Mrs. Grizzel Apthorp, the mother of the first rector. It is ordinarily used only on special occasions.

Batchelder, *ibid.*, p. 69.

Appendix G

The Prayer Used by Colonel Palfrey in the New Year's Eve Service for General and Mrs. Washington, December 31, 1775

O Lord our Heavenly Father, high and mighty, King of kings and Lord of lords, who hast made of one blood all the nations upon earth, and whose common bounty is liberally bestowed upon thy unworthy creatures; most heartily we beseech Thee to look down with mercy upon his Majesty George the Third. Open his eyes and enlighten his understanding, that he may pursue the true interest of the people over whom Thou in thy Providence hast placed him. Remove far from him all wicked, corrupt men, and evil counsellors, that his throne may be established in justice and righteousness; and so replenish him with the grace of thy Holy Spirit, that he may incline to thy will and walk in thy way.

Have pity, O most merciful Father, upon the distresses of the inhabitants of this western world. To that end we humbly pray Thee to bless the Continental Congress. Preside over their councils, and may they be led to such measures as may tend to thy glory, to the advancement of people. We also pray Thee to bless our provincial assemblies, magistrates, and all in subordinate places of power and trust. Be with thy servant the Commander-in-chief of the American forces. Afford him thy presence in all his undertakings; strengthen him that he may vanquish and overcome all his enemies; and grant that we may in due time be restored to the enjoyment of those inestimable blessings we have been deprived of by the devices of cruel and bloodthirsty men, for the sake of thy Son, Jesus Christ our Lord. Amen.

Batchelder, *ibid.*, p. 42.

APPENDIX H

DR. LANGDON'S LAST YEARS —
AN EPISODE IN THE HISTORY OF CHURCH UNITY

In 1891 at the age of sixty Dr. Langdon retired from parochial ministry and went to live with one of his sons in Providence, R.I., in order to give himself completely to his chief passion, namely, Christian unity and particularly a union between the Episcopal and the Presbyterian Churches. To further this end he founded a fellowship entitled The League of Catholic Unity, of which he was the first secretary, "whose purpose was to devote itself to sympathetic study of the possibilities of interdenominational union and the furtherance, as they shall become wise and sure, of active steps toward the reuniting of organic Christendom."

Meanwhile, a commission of our General Convention with which Dr. Langdon kept in constant touch had been appointed and had sent an invitation to about twenty different Protestant Churches to enter into brotherly conference in an attempt to effect the restoration of the organic unity of the Protestant Church. It is interesting in the light of Twentieth Century events in the field of church unity to note that while the various churches responded politely, the warmest response came from the Presbyterian Church and with them the Commission carried on a considerable correspondence. This correspondence with the Presbyterian Church was the most hopeful approach toward unity that our Church had made up to that time. The Commission presented an enthusiastic report at the General Convention in 1895 stressing their belief that "the agitation of the questions connected with Christian Unity has done untold good in attracting the thought of the age to the evil and sin of schism and in arousing discussion concerning methods to put an end to strife and division amongst men who profess to follow the Prince of Peace Who hath taught us that the Church is His one body." The Commission further had a memorial from the Diocese of Indiana urging that it invite all interested churches to take part in a general conference on the question of church unity on the basis of the Lambeth quadrilateral.

Dr. Langdon undoubtedly looked forward to the Commission's being instructed to follow through with the approach made with the Presbyterians and also to the calling of this general conference. Unfortunately, however, the General Convention was a great disappointment to those who believed in unity. It voted to lay on the table the request for a general conference of churches and simply continued the Commission without any general instructions to consult further with the Presbyterians. Consequently, we read in the National Encyclopedia of American Biography "that the retrogressive attitude taken by the Protestant Episcopal General Convention of 1895 put to an end for the time any progress in the direction of unity and that the keen disappointment over the result proved the last straw on Dr. Langdon's exhausted strength and he died a few days afterwards on October 29, 1895." It also states that his funeral at Grace Church, Providence, on All Saints' Day was attended by some thirty-five clergymen of eleven different denominations who partook of the Holy Communion together. Surely this was an appropriate and indeed a beautiful way of closing the door on a life of one who pioneered in the field of church unity at a time when divisions were marked by high and thick walls of differing doctrine, long standing prejudices, and acrimonious feelings. The sad fact is that all this might well be dated 1946 instead of 1895.

Appendix I

Senior Wardens of Christ Church

1762	David Phips
1763	John Vassall
1764	Robert Temple
1766	David Phips
1767	Thomas Oliver
1771	John Vassall
1772	Ezekiel Lewis
1773	Joseph Lee
1774	David Phips
1791	Jonathan Sampson, Jr.
1796	John Trecothick Apthorp
1800	Samuel Wyllis Pomeroy
1801	Abraham Biglow
1802	Richard Richardson
1804	William Winthrop
1814	Abraham Biglow
1829	Joseph Foster
1836	Samuel P. P. Fay
1841	Charles C. Foster
1842	Isaac Lum
1844	Clark Gayton Pickman
1847	William Cranch Bond
1852	Henry L. Eustis
1852	Luther Foote
1852	George Phillips Bond
1860	Herbert H. Stimpson
1861	Luther Crane
1862	Herbert H. Stimpson
1864	Abraham Edwards
1865	Samuel Batchelder, Jr.
1879	George Dexter
1880	Samuel Batchelder, Jr.
1888	Francis Charles Foster
1892	Sturgis Hooper Thorndike
1893	Benjamin D. Washburn
1895	Francis Charles Foster
1901	Albert D. S. Bell
1907	Joseph H. Beale
1921	Stoughton Bell
1932	Henry R. Brigham
1933	Stoughton Bell
1936	James Garfield

JUNIOR WARDENS OF CHRIST CHURCH

1762	John Vassall
1763	Robert Temple
1764	Richard Lechmere
1766	Thomas Oliver
1767	John Vassall
1771	Ezekiel Lewis
1772	John Fenton
1772	Jonathan Sewall
1774	John Pigeon
1791	Nathaniel Bethune
1796	Andrew Craigie
1800	Abraham Biglow
1801	Richard Richardson
1801	Andrew Craigie
1802	Jonathan Bird
1804	Ebenezer Stedman, Jr.
1810	Abraham Biglow
1814	Samuel P. P. Fay
1816	William Dandridge Peck
1820	J. R. Dana
1821	Jonathan Hearsey
1826	Samuel P. P. Fay
1829	Abraham Biglow
1833	Samuel P. P. Fay
1836	Isaac Lum
1841	James Greenleaf
1842	Edward Hyde
1843	Luther Foote
1844	Charles Chase
1845	William Edwards Carter
1852	Richard H. Dana, Jr.
1852	John Montgomery Batchelder
1853	Charles F. Foster
1860	Luther Crane
1861	Samuel Batchelder, Jr.
1865	John Gardner White
1872	Joseph Fay Greenough
1873	William A. Herrick
1875	John Gardner White
1877	Francis Charles Foster
1878	Samuel D. Sargeant
1879	Lucius L. Hubbard
1883	William W. Manning
1884	James Greenleaf Croswell
1887	Frederick Stanhope Hill
1893	William E. Wall

1895   Benjamin D. Washburn
1898   Albert D. S. Bell
1901   Thomas A. Jaggar, Jr.
1906   Joseph H. Beale
1907   Huntington Saville
1919   Hammond V. Hayes
1921   Henry R. Brigham
1932   Francis B. Sayre
1933   Clarence H. Poor
1936   Frank H. Golding
1940   Calvert Magruder

CLERKS OF CHRIST CHURCH PARISH

CLERK AND SEXTON

1763   Thomas Sherren
1774   Joseph Welch

CLERK

1794   James Fillebrown
1817   Abraham Biglow
1833   Henry F. McGee
1838   Thomas G. Wells
1839   William Torrey
1840   James Greenleaf
1842   Edward Hyde
1843   Luther Foote
1844   Elijah Fiske

CLERK, TREASURER, AND COLLECTOR

1847   George Phillips Bond
1851   Francis Lowell Batchelder

CLERK AND TREASURER

1856   James C. Merrill
1862   Francis Charles Foster
1864   James C. Merrill
1865   Alfred Whitman
1866   Francis W. Story
1866   William Wright
1867   Alfred Whitman
1869   George Dexter
1872   David Greene Haskins
1873   Henry P. Walcott
1873   John M. Whittemore, Jr.
1873   George C. Wright
1874   John W. T. Nichols
1875   Thomas Potts James
1876   John M. Whittemore, Jr.

| 1878 | Simon Greenleaf Croswell |
| 1879 | Henry H. Elliott |

PARISH AND VESTRY CLERK

1880	Simon Greenleaf Croswell
1885	James J. Greenough
1888	Edward C. Wright
1889	Sturgis H. Thorndike
1892	Huntington Saville
1900	Samuel F. Batchelder
1927	Roberts Tunis
1934	Allyn Bailey Forbes
1947	Erwin Schell

PARISH TREASURERS

In the early years the Senior Warden was apparently the Treasurer. From 1847 to 1879 the Clerk was also Treasurer. In 1880 the two positions were separated and Mr. George Dexter was the first to hold the position of Parish Treasurer.

1880	S. G. Croswell
1888	F. Stanhope Hill
1893	H. D. Wright
1896	F. Stanhope Hill
1910	Hammond V. Hayes

From 1911 to 1942 in addition to the Parish Treasurer there was also a Missionary Treasurer.

PARISH TREASURERS

1911 — Hammond V. Hayes
1916 — Henry R. Brigham
1918 — Huntington P. Faxon
1925 — Thomas W. Little
1932 — Paul Gring
1935 — Henry DeC. Ward
1936 — Walcott B. Thompson

MISSIONARY TREASURERS

1911 — John Sturgis
1917 — Huntington P. Faxon
1920 — Cushing Toppan
1931 — Dorr Viele
1932 — Henry M. Shreve
        Richard C. Evarts
1933 — George L. Dow
1936 — Humphrey J. Emery
1938 — Frederick G. Kileski
1942 — Walcott B. Thompson

ASSISTANT TREASURERS

1931 — William B. Gentleman
1933 — Walcott B. Thompson
1936 — Richard W. Simmers
1937 — Norman A. Dill
1950 — Manning A. Williams, Jr.

THE VESTRY ASSOCIATION [1]

The Vestry Association consists of all former members of the vestry now living, irrespective of whether or not they are still members of the parish.

Park Appel
Herbert Barry
Stoughton Bell
Richard H. Blasdale
William H. Boardman
Roswell Blair
Henry R. Brigham
Hans L. Carstensen
Norman Dill
Dows Dunham
Roger W. Eckfeldt
Seymour P. Edgerton
James V. D. Eppes
Richard C. Evarts
Stanley G. H. Fitch
Maxwell Fish
Charles S. Gardner
Roger Gilman
Murray Hall
S. Park Harman
Shelby Harrington
Hammond V. Hayes
Richard Henshaw
Frederick G. Kileski
Hugh R. Leavell

Howard T. Lewis
Thomas W. Little
John M. Maguire
Dudley Merrill
Burton A. Miller
Arthur F. Musgrave
Henry W. Newbegin
Arthur Nichols
Charles C. Peabody
Philip Rhinelander
Arthur T. Row
Joseph B. Russell, Jr.
Paul E. Sabine
Thomas H. Sanders
Francis B. Sayre
Richard W. Simmers
Cecil H. Smith
Warren Stearns
Cushing Toppan
George S. Tucker, Jr.
Lynde W. Tucker
Roberts Tunis
Henry DeC. Ward
Donald Wright

[1] The names of the present vestry appear on page 151.